A Jiffy
for Eternity

Cycle A Sermons for
Lent and Easter
Based on the Gospel Texts

Robert Leslie Holmes

CSS Publishing Company, Inc.
Lima, Ohio

A JIFFY FOR ETERNITY

FIRST EDITION
Copyright © 2013
by CSS Publishing Co., Inc.

Library of Congress Cataloging-in-Publication Data

Holmes, Robert Leslie, 1945-
    A jiffy for eternity : cycle A sermons for Lent and Easter based on the Gospel texts /
Robert Leslie Holmes.
        pages cm
    Includes bibliographical references and index.
    ISBN 0-7880-2762-X (alk. paper)
    1. Bible. Gospels--Sermons. 2. Lenten sermons. 3. Easter--Sermons. 4. Common lectionary (1992). Year A. I. Title.

    BS2555.54.H66 2013
    252'.62--dc23
                                    2013015024

ISBN-13: 978-0-7880-2762-8
ISBN-10: 0-7880-2762-X

PRINTED IN USA

To
all who faithfully proclaim God's word

and once more to
Barbara

Preface

"An obligation is laid on me, and woe to me if I do not proclaim the gospel!" (1 Corinthians 9:16). If you are reading this book there is a good chance that you too have felt your own "obligation" to preach. This is, after all, a book for preachers and is designed to help them with their preaching. Moreover, it is a book written by a preacher who teaches preaching. You and I are, together, the custodians of the most important information this world will ever hear. Every day millions of people across the world tune in for the nightly news on television. Yet we know, as they must know, that the nightly news is delivered by people who almost certainly did not write what they are reading. What is more, the news report will be different tomorrow. The most constant thing about it is that it stays in a state of flux. The message we deliver is different because those who preach it usually also compose it. Moreover, our message never changes. For two millennia now the message has been the same. We are charged to deliver the same essential message in a different envelope every time we preach. That reality presents an extra challenge that few people, outside of preachers, can understand.

This is our message: God loves the world and gave his Son, Jesus, to save it. How many different ways are there to say that? That is our constant challenge. It would be an impossible task were it not for the fact that when we prepare and when we preach, another stands beside us and empowers our message. It is the one who loved us all the way to Calvary and loves us still. In his name, God has entrusted us with an "obligation" about the message that supersedes every other message in the world. In his name, God gives us the Holy Spirit who makes the message we preach new for every generation. In addition, God has given us a book so filled with truths around which to preach that we could never run out of things to say. And so, we preach!

This little volume has been fun to author largely because I love preaching and preachers. I send it forth with the prayer that God will use it to kindle your fire for the pulpit. The Beatles sang, "I get by with a little help from my friends." I suspect that could be a theme song for every preacher. As you might imagine, no one can write a book like this without friends and the stories they share. The seeds that spring forth here as stories are God's gifts to me from a variety of sources. While I have tried to give just credit where it is due, it is possible I have omitted credit that someone believes is rightly his or hers. Be assured that the omission is unintentional and please accept my apologies.

Perhaps you are wondering about its title. After a season of mental wrestling, it seemed that the most effective title for this volume was the same as one of the messages in the book. "A Jiffy for Eternity" also symbolizes the reality that for a limited all-too-short period every week we represent eternal truth to all who come to hear us. Even as I have had fun preparing this manuscript for publication, may you also have fun as you read it and take its message to heart.

The words on these pages are in a lot better shape because my wife, Barbara, has reviewed them. Debra Meyer of Pittsburgh, Pennsylvania, has served me well as my editor. Debra's well-trained eagle eye picked up all kinds of typos and other errors, and all of us are the beneficiaries of her good work. For Barbara's and Debra's encouragement and assistance with this project, I am very grateful. My granddaughter, Cameron Eby, was an especially helpful research assistant. Also deserving of special mention are the people of CSS Publishing who first approached me about doing this project. I appreciate the trust they placed in me and hope they now feel it was not such a bad idea after all. Finally, I am grateful to you, the reader. Without you there would be no need to write this book or any of the others I have written or edited. I pray that you will find in these pages not only ideas for sermons but food to nourish your soul. As you read these words, stop occasionally to remember that you are being prayed for, because you are. May God enrich your life and ministry through what is said here. And may I ask one favor as I close? That is, would you please pray for me when you say your prayers?

Finally, a word for those who read this book with a goal other than preaching: It comes to you with my special prayer that God will use its message to strengthen your life and enrich your walk with him. May you find here food that nourishes your soul in Christ's service.

Soli Deo Gloria!

— Robert Leslie Holmes
Augusta, Georgia
(Philippians 1:9-11)

Table of Contents

Ash Wednesday   9
Are You Sorry Enough to Wash Your Face?
Matthew 6:1-6, 16-21

Lent 1   19
Jesus or Niccolò?
Matthew 4:1-11

Lent 2   31
A Jiffy for Eternity!
John 3:1-17

Lent 3   43
The Womb of Amazing Grace!
John 4:5-42

Lent 4   55
Here's Mud in Your Eye!
John 9:1-41

Lent 5   65
When Lazarus Leaped and Laughed!
John 11:1-45

Passion / Palm Sunday   75
Live Spelled Backward!
Matthew 26:14—27:66

Maundy Thursday   85
No Greater Love!
John 13:1-17, 31b-35

Good Friday   95
Son of a Daddy!
John 18:1—19:42

Easter Sunday   105
Oh Say, Can You See By the Dawn's Early Light?
John 20:1-18

Easter 2   115
Afraid of Hope!
John 20:19-31

Easter 3   125
When Heartbreak Turns to Heartburn!
Luke 24:13-35

Easter 4   135
The Gate to Grace, Goodness, and Glory
John 10:1-10

Easter 5   145
The Power of the Trust Factor
John 14:1-14

Easter 6   155
This Spirit Is Not Spooky
John 14:15-21

Ascension of Our Lord   165
The Time Is Now!
Luke 24:44-53

Easter 7   175
The Biggest Prayer Ever Prayed Under Heaven!
John 17:1-11

If You Like This Book...   185

Are You Sorry Enough to Wash Your Face?

Beware of practicing your piety before others in order to be seen by them; for then you have no reward from your Father in heaven. So whenever you give alms, do not sound a trumpet before you, as the hypocrites do in the synagogues and in the streets, so that they may be praised by others. Truly I tell you, they have received their reward. But when you give alms, do not let your left hand know what your right hand is doing, so that your alms may be done in secret; and your Father who sees in secret will reward you. And whenever you pray, do not be like the hypocrites; for they love to stand and pray in the synagogues and at the street corners, so that they may be seen by others. Truly I tell you, they have received their reward. But whenever you pray, go into your room and shut the door and pray to your Father who is in secret; and your Father who sees in secret will reward you... And whenever you fast, do not look dismal, like the hypocrites, for they disfigure their faces so as to show others that they are fasting. Truly I tell you, they have received their reward. But when you fast, put oil on your head and wash your face, so that your fasting may be seen not by others but by your Father who is in secret; and your Father who sees in secret will reward you. Do not store up for yourselves treasures on earth, where moth and rust consume and where thieves break in and steal; but store up for yourselves treasures in heaven, where neither moth nor rust consumes and where thieves do not break in and steal. For where your treasure is, there your heart will be also.

For Christians around the world, Ash Wednesday is the first day of Lent. It was the practice among early Roman

Christians for penitents to begin their period of public penance on the first day of Lent. They were sprinkled with ashes, dressed in sackcloth, and obliged to remain away from fellowship with other people until they reconciled with fellow Christians on Maundy Thursday, the day before Good Friday and three days before Easter, the day of resurrection.

Ash Wednesday is ultimately about one of the biggest words in the Bible. That word is not a great big word in terms of its length for there are many longer words both in English and in New Testament Greek. This word is big in terms of its depth of meaning. It was the theme John the Baptist preached and we read: "In those days John the Baptist appeared in the wilderness of Judea, proclaiming, 'Repent, for the kingdom of heaven has come near'" (Matthew 3:1-2). The same word is found in the opening line of Jesus' first sermon: "Jesus began to proclaim, 'Repent, for the kingdom of heaven has come near'" (Matthew 4:17). The same word and the idea it conveys and the action that it calls for were at the heart of the apostle Paul's preaching: "I declared first to those in Damascus, then in Jerusalem and throughout the countryside of Judea, and also to the Gentiles, that they should repent and turn to God and do deeds consistent with repentance" (Acts 26:20). That word that Jesus, John the Baptist, and Paul preached appears 75 times in the Bible. You have figured by now, I trust, that I speak of the word "Repent!" Ash Wednesday is primarily about repentance.

The primary Greek New Testament word for repentance brings together two Greek words. The first means "to turn around" and the second means "your mind." Hence, the Greek word for repent means "turn around your way of thinking." The Bible calls for a process of four steps to make that a life reality.

The first step is regret. Paul writes, "Godly grief produces a repentance that leads to salvation and brings no regret" (2 Corinthians 7:10). Regret means a recognition that something wrong has occurred or that something right has not occurred.

On May 6, 1954, Roger Bannister became the first man in history to run a mile in less than 4 minutes. Within two months, John Landy eclipsed the record by 1.4 seconds. On August 7, 1954, the two met for a historic race. As they moved into the last lap, Landy held the lead. To the cheering crowd, it looked as if Landy had the race in the bag. Then an amazing thing happened. As he neared the finish line, Landy was haunted by the question, "Where is Roger?" In an instant, John Landy turned to look back and as he did Roger Bannister took the lead. At a press conference following that race, John Landy said, "I had it. Had I not looked back, I would have won!" It was an acknowledgment that his action led to a bad outcome for him. Regret is the intellectual admission that you did something you should not have done. Regret forces us to admit to ourselves, "I was wrong."

The second step is remorse. "Godly grief produces a repentance that leads to salvation and brings no regret" (2 Corinthians 7:10). The emotion of grief has its place in repentance so now we have regret, which is intellectual, and remorse, which is emotional. Remorse happens when intellect and emotion unite in shame.

Jesus told a parable of contrast about a Pharisee, the personification of the hypocrite in our Ash Wednesday scripture reading, who prayed with a high sense of himself and a tax collector who was filled with remorse. "God," said the Pharisee, "I thank you that I am not like other men. I fast twice a week and give a tenth of everything I get." The tax collector, on the other hand, dared not even to look toward heaven but beat upon his breast as he pleaded, "God have mercy on me. I'm a sinner!" One said, "I'm a front pew religionist." The other countered, "I'm not even worthy of entering the service."

Catch the emotion of the latter man's confession! That's

11

remorse! It is that emotional sense that I not only know intellectually that I am guilty and I feel a sense of deep shame for who I am and what I have done, but in my soul I feel my guilt and the consequences of my sin. That is remorse, the second component of repentance.

The third component of repentance is a return to God. "I declared first to those in Damascus, then in Jerusalem and throughout the countryside of Judea, and also to the Gentiles, that they should repent and turn to God…" (Acts 26:20). This is the heart of Ash Wednesday and Lent.

Imagine that you are on the road to a destination and you realize that the pathway you have traveled, rather than taking you toward where you want to end up is actually taking you away from your desired destination. Your GPS keeps directing you to "make a legal U-turn." This is the absolute essence of repentance; it recognizes that you are headed the wrong way and need to turn back around. Ash Wednesday is the great turn-around day on the Christian calendar.

Repentance calls for our return to the ways of the gospel of Jesus and for the removal of focus on ourselves. That is the sum and substance of Matthew's words in this scripture reading. Listen again:

> Beware of practicing your piety before others in order to be seen by them… Whenever you give alms, do not sound a trumpet before you, as the hypocrites do in the synagogues and in the streets, so that they may be praised by others… When you give alms, do not let your left hand know what your right hand is doing, so that your alms may be done in secret; and your Father who sees in secret will reward you. And whenever you pray, do not be like the hypocrites; for they love to stand and pray in the synagogues and at the street corners, so that they may be seen by others… Whenever you pray, go into your room and shut the door and pray to your Father who is in secret… And whenever you fast, do not look dismal, like the hypocrites, for they disfigure their faces so as to show others that they are fasting… But when you fast, put oil on your head and wash

your face, so that your fasting may be seen not by others but by your Father who is in secret; and your Father who sees in secret will reward you.
(vv. 1-6, 16-18)

Did you hear that? "…when you fast, put oil on your head and wash your face, so that your fasting may be seen not by others" (v. 17). True repentance is not about public display but about a secret relationship between believers and the all-seeing God.

What does this say about Ash Wednesday ashes? Do you know there is not a word about Ash Wednesday ashes anywhere in the Bible? Jesus neither spoke about nor practiced it. His disciples did not do it. The early church did not administer ashes. When and where, then, did this practice of Ash Wednesday ashes begin?

To be sure there are biblical references to ashes. King David's daughter, Tamar, is one example. After Tamar was sexually violated by her half-brother, Amnon, we read, "Tamar put ashes on her head, and tore the long robe that she was wearing; she put her hand on her head, and went away, crying aloud as she went" (2 Samuel 13:19). But will you note that it was not Tamar's sin but the cultural shame of her time that caused her so to act? That is not the same as Lenten repentance today.

Then there is Mordecai's reaction to Haman's decree as recorded in Esther 4:1-3. Mordecai felt personally responsible for what happened but there is no indicator that Mordecai's response was because of great faith in God for there is no mention of God and no record of accompanying prayer. It was, if anything, a psychological reaction to a national downturn. Again it is not about anything like biblical repentance.

Then we read about Job's dust and ashes repentance in his amazing acknowledgment to God: "I had heard of you by the hearing of the ear, but now my eye sees you; therefore I despise myself, and repent in dust and ashes" (Job 42:5-6). Job, changing the tenor of his previous calls, recognized that his earlier cries for explanation now paled in significance to his personal encounter with the almighty. This was something greater than he had before imagined. Once he was focused on what he lost but now he found God. His losses paled when compared to what he found. It is one of the most dramatic encounters in all scripture but it does not tie into Ash Wednesday ashes.

Finally, we have two references to penance and ashes from Jeremiah's prophecy: "O my poor people, put on sackcloth, and roll in ashes; make mourning as for an only child, most bitter lamentation: for suddenly the destroyer will come upon us" (Jeremiah 6:26).

"Wail, you shepherds, and cry out; roll in ashes, you lords of the flock, for the days of your slaughter have come — and your dispersions, and you shall fall like a choice vessel" (Jeremiah 25:34).

The similarities are as significant as the difference. First, because of the specified action: Each is a call to "roll in ashes" not to place ashes on the head of the penitents. Second: Each is a future tense warning about what will happen if the current national practices continue and not an individual past tense sorrow for sins already completed.

So how and where did forehead ashes become the church's Ash Wednesday symbol? As we have just seen, this tradition does not find roots in biblical example. While the exact origin of the day is not clear, the custom of marking the head with ashes on this day is said to have originated during the papacy of Gregory the Great, which church history records ran from 590 to 604 AD. Originally, the use of forehead ashes as a mark of penance was a matter of private devotion. It was carried out in private with no witnesses. Only the presiding clergy and the penitent were witnesses.

Later it became part of the official rite for reconciling public penitents.

The practice may not even have originally been birthed in the church. Prior to the birth of Pope Gregory, there is evidence that ancient Romans celebrated the festival of Lupercalia in mid-February. Lupercalia was a festival of debauchery where archaic gods who permitted indulgence in sensual pleasures, scandalous activities including wife swapping (without regard for a wife's emotions), and drunkenness without inhibition were worshiped. It may be that somewhere between the fifth century and eighth century, the pre-Reformation church determined that church members could participate in Lupercalia and make amends with confession of sin and payment of an indulgence tax called "penance" to the church. When penance was paid, ashes on the head of the "penitent" were a way of signifying to the outside world that the sinner had made amends. Of course, next year they could do it all over again!

The Reformers Calvin, Luther, Knox, Hus, Melanchthon, and Zwingli all condemned the practice of Lupercalia and paying for indulgences. Why? Because it ran totally counter to scripture! We see this is today's scripture when Jesus likens repentance to being cleansed, not dirtied up! "Wash your face!" he says. For Christians, true repentance is more than an annual mark on the head. It is a daily mark on the heart, "… not (to) be seen by others but by your Father who is in secret… your Father who sees in secret will reward you" (v. 18).

I know that some of us are from different backgrounds, and I respect that. Yet scripture says that we are people of a joyful countenance not a dirty face: "When you fast, put oil on your head and wash your face, so that your fasting may be seen not by others but by your Father who is in secret; and your Father who sees in secret will reward you" (v. 18). So, whether or not you receive ashes, make very sure that your motivation is not about yourself but about the glory of Jesus.

Are you sorry enough to wash your face? Are you prepared to acknowledge where you have been wrong, to demonstrate true remorse, and to change your ways and return to the ways of Jesus? That, my friends, is the essence of repentance. Repentance is what Ash Wednesday is all about. In Isaiah's words, "Seek the Lord while he may be found, call upon him while he is near; let the wicked forsake their way, and the unrighteous their thoughts; let them return to the Lord, that he may have mercy on them, and to our God, for he will abundantly pardon. For my thoughts are not your thoughts, nor are your ways my ways, says the Lord" (Isaiah 55:6-8).

Finally, repentance calls for a return to the ways of Jesus. "I declared first to those in Damascus, then in Jerusalem and throughout the countryside of Judea, and also to the Gentiles, that they should… do deeds consistent with repentance" (Acts 26:20).

Repentance is about choosing a new life pathway and setting out in a different direction from the way we were going before. It is bigger than one day. True repentance is demonstrated over a lifetime.

When King Uzziah died, Isaiah entered the temple and saw the Lord of glory there, and he was immediately conscious of his sinfulness: "And I said: 'Woe is me! I am lost, for I am a man of unclean lips, and I live among a people of unclean lips; yet my eyes have seen the king, the Lord of hosts!' Then one of the seraphs flew to me, holding a live coal that had been taken from the altar with a pair of tongs. The seraph touched my mouth with it and said: 'Now that this has touched your lips, your guilt has departed and your sin is blotted out' " (Isaiah 6:5-7).

In that encounter, the old Isaiah died and the new Isaiah came to life with a mission that would touch God's people forevermore. We hear the joy of his call in these words: "I heard the voice of the Lord saying, 'Whom shall I send, and who will go for us?' And I said, 'Here am I; send me!' " (Isaiah 6:8). The old Isaiah had a new life and a new mission. That is what repentance does.

When Saul of Tarsus did business with the resurrected Jesus Christ on the Damascus Road, he could never return to his old paths. The old Saul died that day and was reborn as the greatest apostle of Christendom.

Zacchaeus is another example of true repentance in action. Scrambling down from his sycamore tree perch to Jesus, Zacchaeus said, "Look, half of my possessions, Lord, I will give to the poor; and if I have defrauded anyone of anything, I will pay back four times as much." Then Jesus said to him, "Today salvation has come to this house, because he too is a son of Abraham" (Luke 19:8-9). Zacchaeus knew that the cost of making his sin right would forever be less than leaving it wrong. What is true for Zacchaeus is true even now for you and me.

Are you ready to join the people of joyful countenance and not a dirty face? Are you sorry enough to "wash your face"? Hear the greatest news we can ever know: "Let the wicked forsake their way, and the unrighteous their thoughts; let them return to the Lord, that he may have mercy on them, and to our God, for he will abundantly pardon" (Isaiah 55:7). It is still gloriously true and that is the wonder of Lent.

Jesus or Niccolò?

Then Jesus was led up by the Spirit into the wilderness to be tempted by the devil. He fasted forty days and forty nights, and afterwards he was famished. The tempter came and said to him, "If you are the Son of God, command these stones to become loaves of bread." But he answered, "It is written, 'One does not live by bread alone, but by every word that comes from the mouth of God.' " Then the devil took him to the holy city and placed him on the pinnacle of the temple, saying to him, "If you are the Son of God, throw yourself down; for it is written, 'He will command his angels concerning you,' and 'On their hands they will bear you up, so that you will not dash your foot against a stone.' " Jesus said to him, "Again it is written, 'Do not put the Lord your God to the test.' " Again, the devil took him to a very high mountain and showed him all the kingdoms of the world and their splendor; and he said to him, "All these I will give you, if you will fall down and worship me." Jesus said to him, "Away with you, Satan! for it is written, 'Worship the Lord your God, and serve only him.' " Then the devil left him, and suddenly angels came and waited on him.

This world's kingdoms have never been presented in a more Machiavellian fashion or more compellingly. And never before and never again have they been nor will they be targeted to one with more reason to succumb. Surely one of the great strengthening comforts of taking Jesus Christ as our Lord is that he, more than anyone else, understands our temptations. Scripture tells us, "He himself was tested by what he suffered, he is able to help those who are being tested" (Hebrews 2:18). So we can say with confidence that we do not follow an out-of-touch Savior. As the Bible tells us, "We do not have a high priest who is unable to sympathize with our weaknesses, but we have one who in every respect has been tested as we are, yet without sin. Let us therefore approach the throne of grace with boldness, so that we may receive mercy and find grace to help in time of need" (Hebrews 4:15-16).

Is Jesus really that good, you may ask? Come with me to the primary pivotal moment in the life of Jesus Christ. This moment demonstrates not only that he is, in fact, that good but that he also is the most morally fit leader the world has ever known and strong enough to reign as our King of kings and Lord of lords. If Christ's genealogy and virgin birth are sufficient evidence to establish his legal human right to serve as Israel's king and if that heavenly baptismal declaration, "This is my beloved Son" establishes the Father's affirmation of his true identity, then his temptation experience demonstrates just how strong his righteousness is for everyday living. This Jesus in Matthew's gospel stands before the world as God's unique Holy Spirit-empowered Son. Each of his temptations tests his devotion to the Father. It clearly is Satan's intention to undermine all these things. Should the devil prove successful at doing this he will destroy everything that Jesus is and undo God's plan for the redemption of his people.

Furthermore, from each temptation we can learn how it is that Jesus understands our testing times and how we can be more successful in facing down our own temptations. This passage opens to us two points.

First, studying Jesus' temptations makes us aware of the devil's devious ways. In Matthew 4, the same Holy Spirit who caused Jesus to be conceived in the womb of his virgin mother (as reported in Matthew 1:20) and who (according to Matthew 3:16) descended like a dove to demonstrate the Father's approval of him, now leads God's Son into the wilderness of temptation.

Let's pause for a moment and think about the significance of the place where Jesus was tempted. This is, so far as we know, the same wilderness where John the Baptist once proclaimed his message of repentance and the coming kingdom. Earlier Hosea recorded for us that the wilderness was the setting for God's reaffirmation of the unique forever-love relationship between himself and Israel. Bible history records that God once before announced his love for these people, even though they had proven their unfaithfulness to him in many ways. In Hosea 2:14-23 God's power and grace is restated to them in a new wilderness hike.

Now Jesus, who came among us as the personal demonstration of that love, comes to the wilderness to be tempted. Actually the Greek word *peirazo* that is translated "tempted" here is amorphous. It can mean to tempt or to test in either a good or bad sense. Using the same Greek word, scripture repeatedly assures us that God does not test anyone. This is never clearer than in James 1:13, which straightforwardly tells us that "no one, when tempted, should say, 'I am being tempted by God'; for God... himself tempts no one."

Having said this, let there be no doubt that God does allow us to be tested by the world, the flesh, and the devil. Consider, for example, these words:

> Do not love the world or the things in the world. The love of the Father is not in those who love the world; for all that is in the world — the desire of the flesh, the desire of the eyes, the pride in riches — comes not from the Father but from the world. And the world and its desire are passing away, but those who do the will of God live for ever.
> (1 John 2:15-17)

Remember, too, Saint Paul's anguish from his words in the second half of Romans 7, when he says among other things, "I find it to be a law that when I want to do what is good, evil lies close at hand" (Romans 7:21). Spiritually speaking, it is not being too harsh to say that Paul was a walking civil war. Perhaps you can identify with what he writes here. Hence, we can say that while God does not tempt us, clearly God does allow temptations to follow us. God the Holy Spirit clearly led Jesus into the wilderness, which would become Christ's place of temptation where the devil went to work on him!

It was a moment of danger for the newly baptized Lord. "He fasted forty days and forty nights, and afterwards he was famished" (v. 2). Wouldn't we all be famished? Fasting in scripture was a mark of refraining from physical nourishment to focus on the spiritual life. Two of the great Old Testament characters, Moses and Elijah, knew firsthand the experience of a forty-day fast, according to Exodus 34:28 and 1 Kings 19:8, so this was an elite spiritual fraternity with whom the Lord Jesus perhaps felt a special connection — you may recall that these two appeared with Jesus later in his ministry on the Mount of Transfiguration. From what Luke the physician says (see Luke 4:2), it seems safe to conclude that the only thing that crossed Jesus' lips for those forty days of fasting was water. Mark, recalling this moment in Jesus' life, points out that while Jesus was not eating, there were wild animals around and angels waited on him (see Mark 1:13). Despite the concerns that come with extraordinary hunger and the presence of those wild animals, Jesus, surely physically weak was still spiritually and mentally strong. Forty days of fasting in the presence of wild animals would not and could not force him to succumb to Satan's fiery darts. The devil's darts were focused on three particular areas. Since we also face temptation in these three areas, let us consider each of them.

Intellectually, Satan could imagine what a lack of food for a prolonged period would do to someone and so it should not come as a surprise to learn that the devil's first temptation is directed toward Jesus' physical vulnerability. The wily Satan begins with a double-pronged attack that questions Christ's identity while suggesting a quick fix to his current physical needs. "If you are the Son of God, command these stones to become loaves of bread" (v. 3). Let me paraphrase, "With one quick move, you can prove who you really are, the Son of God, and just what you are capable of doing; you can turn stones into bread." Satan knew exactly the true identity of Jesus. The preface to his temptation to make bread out of stones was not designed to question the Lord's identity but to suggest that this was a moment of opportunity to prove that Jesus could do something without the concurrence of his Father, thus undermining his earthly mission.

Jesus puts the kibosh on Satan's attack not as God, but as a man. With no denial that he is, in fact, hungry and could make stones into bread, Jesus employs a power that any one of us can use. It is the power of God's word. Obedience to the word of God outshines, and therefore beats, self-grati-fying directed temptations every time, even over such basic needs as daily food. "It is written," Jesus tells the devil. "One does not live by bread alone, but by every word that comes from the mouth of God" (v. 4). He quotes scripture Satan must surely know from the restatement of God's law in Deuteronomy 8:3: "He humbled you by letting you hunger, then by feeding you with manna, with which neither you nor your ancestors were acquainted, in order to make you understand that one does not live by bread alone, but by every word that comes from the mouth of the Lord." The message is easy to see: There is far more to life than merely fulfilling physical desires. It has many applications for each of our lives.

Satan's second tempting attack is directed toward the appetite of power and control and is far more bold than the first one: Then the devil took him to the holy city and placed him on the pinnacle of the temple, saying to him, "If you are the Son of God, throw yourself down; for it is written,

'He will command his angels concerning you,' and 'On their hands they will bear you up, so that you will not dash your foot against a stone' " (vv. 5-6). Matthew speaks of the capital city not as Jerusalem but as "the holy city." For Jews, the city of Jerusalem was even more than the capital city of Israel; it was the center of the known world. They remembered Ezekiel 5:5, "Thus says the Lord God: This is Jerusalem; I have set her in the center of the nations, with countries all around her." Satan knows that too and his ploy in this temptation implies that giving in now could bring Jesus international recognition. What is more, Satan "sweetens the pot" now by boldly making a direct reference to a phrase from Psalm 91:11-12: "It is written, 'He will command his angels concerning you to guard you in all your ways. On their hands they will bear you up, so that you will not dash your foot against a stone.' " Think about what is happening here: Bold, crooked Satan would go so far as to use God's own word against God's own Son! Satan's quote is correct insofar as it goes. God does promise that the angels will protect anyone who trusts him; this of necessity now would include Jesus on earth in human flesh. However, Satan's misapplication of scripture takes a text out of context and is, therefore, a pretext! He was tempting the Lord Jesus to act as if the Father existed to serve him instead of the other way around. The children of Israel once had fallen for this satanic ploy, as we read back in Exodus 17. They did not know what Jesus knew: that it is always wrong to expect God to demonstrate his faithfulness by fulfilling his promises on our terms. Testing God is not trusting God. It is playing a game we cannot win.

Jesus does not argue about being God's Son but once more responds to Satan's temptation by applying God's word to the devil's scheme. The one great difference is that Jesus does so with integrity, for he knows the word in context and now is a man under the authority of what God's word says: "Do not put the Lord your God to the test" (v. 7, cf. Deuteronomy 6:16).

In Satan's third temptation, he takes Jesus "to a very high mountain and showed him all the kingdoms of the world and their splendor; and he said to him, 'All these I will give you, if you will fall down and worship me' " (vv. 8-9). With the third temptation, as with the second, it is hard to tell whether Satan physically transported Jesus or simply presented a vision. Luke sheds some light on this: "The devil led him up and showed him in an instant all the kingdoms of the world" (Luke 4:5). If it happened "in an instant" as Luke says, it seems to indicate that it was a visionary trip. Regardless, whether the transportation was physical or visionary is not important for the moment. What is important to remember is that like the first two, this temptation also has eternal implications combined with instant gratification. John's prologue introduces Jesus using, among others, these words: "All things came into being through him, and without him not one thing came into being" (John 1:3). What originally belongs to Christ as this world's Creator, and what the Father promises, according to Psalm 2, he shall inherit as Messiah. Satan, in one of the biggest ruse attempts of all time, now promises to give him what is already his. In other words, Satan promises something Jesus already possesses.

Like the first two temptations, this one also tests Jesus' loyalty to the Father. Had Jesus taken the devil's bait, the whole gospel that saves us would go away in an instant and Jesus would have joined Satan as this world's ruler so that forevermore, Jesus would have ruled as Satan's slave-prince. However, it was not to be and, for a third time, Jesus uses scripture to rebuff and now to dismiss his tempter: "Away with you, Satan! for it is written, 'Worship the Lord your God, and serve only him.' Then the devil left him, and suddenly angels came and waited on him" (vv. 10-11). This would not be the last time the unrelenting Satan would try to tempt Jesus. After Jesus tells the disciples about his forth-coming death, the devil speaks through Peter and Jesus responds sharply, "He turned and said to Peter, 'Get behind me, Satan! You are a stumbling block to me; for you are setting your mind not on divine things but on human things'" (Matthew 16:23). Nonetheless, after these first temptations Jesus now is ready to begin his earthly ministry. Studying Jesus' temptations makes us aware of the devil's devious ways.

Let us now consider some similarities between Christ's experiences of temptation and our own. How all this fits into our everyday world in this time is instructive. First, we need to see and understand that today we face the same enemy Jesus faced in the wilderness. Peter tells us, "Discipline yourselves, keep alert. Like a roaring lion your adversary the devil prowls around, looking for someone to devour. Resist him, steadfast in your faith, for you know that your brothers and sisters in all the world are undergoing the same kinds of suffering" (1 Peter 5:8-9). Forget those jokes you have heard about Satan. He is not that cute little horn-headed fellow who wears a red suit and carries a pitchfork that you may have seen in cartoon pictures. "For our struggle is not against enemies of blood and flesh, but against the rulers, against the authorities, against the cosmic powers of this present darkness, against the spiritual forces of evil in the heavenly places" (Ephesians 6:12).

Second, let us be alert to the fact that Satan's ploys with us will be the same as they were with Jesus. His methods of attack change only in target and venue. In fact, you may have realized that Satan's temptation tactics were essentially the same with Jesus as those he used with Eve in the Garden and are reported in Genesis 3. His three tools of attack are first that he would have us *do* something that is not God's will for us. Second, he will tempt us with the desire to *have* something that is not God's will for us. Third, he will tempt us to *be* something that is not part of God's will for us. John points out his deadly strategy in these words: "For all that is in the world — the desire of the flesh, the desire of the eyes, the pride in riches — comes not from the Father but from the world" (1 John 2:16). Think about this: "The desire of the flesh" is an ungodly inward call to satisfy the things of the body. For Jesus this was hunger. For us it may be either that or something else that is fleshly such as immorality. "The desire of the eyes" can be anything material that runs counter to God's will for us. Finally, he throws at us that fiery dart of "pride in riches." This is the desire to become arrogant or proud through what we own or control.

If you have seen the movie or read the book, you already know that Bilbo Baggins, a fifty-something hobbit, is the main character and protagonist of J.R.R. Tolkien's *The Hobbit*. Hobbits are fictional diminutive humanoids who live in the lands of Middle-earth. Little Bilbo Baggins must cross paths with Smaug, one of the last great dragons of Middle-earth. Fearlessly, Bilbo Baggins creeps into Smaug's dragon-den because his fear is overcome by the lure and lust of Smaug's vast treasure of gold. Calling it "staggerment," Tolkien describes the moment saying that there are no words left to express staggerment…

> Bilbo had heard tell of dragon-hoards before, but the splendor, the lust, the glory of such treasure was something beyond anything he had ever imagined. His heart was filled and pierced with enchantment and with the desire of the little people; and he gazed motionless, almost forgetting the frightful guardian, at the gold beyond price and count.[1]

Whether or not we believe in dragons, we can get caught up in the moment of our temptation. So we need to live out our lives always on the alert, recognizing that God has given us the very same tools Jesus used to overcome Satan's furtive and crafty ways.

As Jesus applied the shield of trust, so must we. Paul calls this taking, "The shield of faith, with which you will be able to quench all the flaming arrows of the evil one" (Ephesians 6:16). As Jesus appealed to God's word, so must we. Paul calls us to take up "the sword of the Spirit, which is the word of God" (Ephesians 6:17). Furthermore, we remember the words of Jesus when he said, "Stay awake and pray that you may not come into the time of trial; the spirit indeed is willing, but the flesh is weak" (Matthew 26:41). Belief in God. The word of God. Pray to God. These are our weapons when temptation comes our way. We decide whether or not to use them.

Here is how it works: Think of the kind of temptation that enters our psyche when our dream promotion is announced at work. We think of ways to get the edge on other potential candidates. Suddenly, there is a temptation to inflate our resume and make claims that are not true. We reason that doing this would give us an advantage over others. We believe that our employer will never find out what we have done and we will get away with it. It happens all the time. The philosophy of sixteenth-century Italian Renaissance politician-humanist Niccolò di Bernardo dei Machiavelli, whom some call the father of situational ethics, kicks into our thinking. A self-focused humanist, Machiavelli encouraged lying, cheating, and even murdering to get ahead where necessary. He advocated trampling over others with no regard for them or truth. Machiavelli recognized cunning deceit and cruelty as character strengths and sometimes-necessary stepping-stones to personal advancement. That is why his name has gone down in infamy as a synonym for devious trickery. I even used a Machiavellian tactic illustratively in the title of this sermon. Had I titled this message, "Jesus or Machiavelli," you would have guessed right away what I had in mind. However, when I used his first name, Niccolò, you probably had no idea what

I had in mind. With this verbal slight of hand, I probably had you fooled until now.

Similarly, Satan will try to fool us with what seems momentarily harmless in his effort to lead us astray from Jesus. When we come to the time of that job promotion opportunity, we may find ourselves thinking on two levels. On one level we ask ourselves, "What would Jesus do?" On another level, we may ask ourselves, "What would Niccolò di Bernardo dei Machiavelli do?" In this moment of temptation, we will decide whether we will follow the example of Jesus Christ or the example of Niccolò Machiavelli. Who will you decide for when that moment comes in your life? Jesus or Niccolò? The way of truth and integrity? Or the way of deceit and craftiness? Make sure you decide well for your very soul is at stake as you make that decision.

In such a moment of temptation, we will find comfort in remembering that we have a Savior high priest who was tempted "at all points as we are" but did not succumb to temptation. For that reason, we worship him today. He went to the cross because he loved us and he loves us still. He understands because he became "like his brothers and sisters in every respect, so that he might be a merciful and faithful high priest in the service of God, to make a sacrifice of atonement for the sins of the people. Because he himself was tested by what he suffered, he is able to help those who are being tested" (Hebrews 2:17-18). What is more, we have the never-ending promise of God's word for us, "We do not have a high priest who is unable to sympathize with our weaknesses, but we have one who in every respect has been tested as we are, yet without sin. Let us therefore approach the throne of grace with boldness, so that we may receive mercy and find grace to help in time of need" (Hebrews 4:15-16).

When temptation comes your way will it be Jesus or Niccolò? The Bible says that we should keep on "looking to Jesus the pioneer and perfecter of our faith, who for the sake of the joy that was set before him endured the cross, disregarding its shame, and has taken his seat at the right hand of the throne of God. Consider him who endured such hostility against himself from sinners, so that you may not grow weary or lose heart" (Hebrews 12:2-3).

Jesus or Niccolò? Who will you follow? Christ or Machiavelli? The eternal destiny of your soul depends on the choices you make when that moment of temptation comes into your life.

---

1. J.R.R. Tolkein, *The Hobbit: Or There and Back Again* (New York: Houghton Mifflin Co., 1966), p. 194.

A Jiffy for Eternity!

Now there was a Pharisee named Nicodemus, a leader of the Jews. He came to Jesus by night and said to him, "Rabbi, we know that you are a teacher who has come from God; for no one can do these signs that you do apart from the presence of God." Jesus answered him, "Very truly, I tell you, no one can see the kingdom of God without being born from above." Nicodemus said to him, "How can anyone be born after having grown old? Can one enter a second time into the mother's womb and be born?" Jesus answered, "Very truly, I tell you, no one can enter the kingdom of God without being born of water and Spirit. What is born of the flesh is flesh, and what is born of the Spirit is spirit. Do not be astonished that I said to you, 'You must be born from above.' The wind blows where it chooses, and you hear the sound of it, but you do not know where it comes from or where it goes. So it is with everyone who is born of the Spirit." Nicodemus said to him, "How can these things be?" Jesus answered him, "Are you a teacher of Israel, and yet you do not understand these things? Very truly, I tell you, we speak of what we know and testify to what we have seen; yet you do not receive our testimony. If I have told you about earthly things and you do not believe, how can you believe if I tell you about heavenly things? No one has ascended into heaven except the one who descended from heaven, the Son of Man. And just as Moses lifted up the serpent in the wilderness, so must the Son of Man be lifted up, that whoever believes in him may have eternal life. For God so loved the world that he gave his only Son, so that everyone who believes in him may not perish but may have eternal life. Indeed, God did not send the Son into the world to condemn the world, but in order that the world might be saved through him."

Character

Sometimes Who's Who doesn't know for sure just what's what! Consider the character of this man who comes to Jesus at night. Nicodemus clearly was a well-connected man yet it is clear he lacks some very vital information. He is remembered here as a "Pharisee," the highest sect among the Jews. We often think of the Pharisees as harsh, hypocritical, and uppity (and certainly there were moments when Jesus heaped scorn on them). Here, however, is a Pharisee, Nicodemus, who does not fit that mold. He is a sincere, mild-mannered personality. This is further confirmed in John 7 when some Pharisees asked the temple police why they had not arrested Jesus. Nicodemus, having already had the dialogue we read in John 3 with Jesus, intercedes by asking, "Our law does not judge people without first giving them a hearing to find out what they are doing, does it?" (John 7:51). When we criticize the Pharisees, let us remember that among them some were, at least one was, motivated by honest and sincere intentions.

In addition to being a Pharisee, it seems likely that Nicodemus is a member of the Sanhedrin, the highest Jewish tribunal, the supreme court of the Jews. He is described as "a leader of the Jews." As a member of both the highest religious and the highest legal group, one might assume that if anybody should know what is going on, it should be Nicodemus. Yet here he comes to Jesus with an open admission that his knowledge is limited and he wants it to grow. Nicodemus says to Jesus, "Rabbi, we know that you are a teacher who has come from God; for no one can do these signs that you do apart from the presence of God" (v. 2). He calls Jesus "rabbi," a title of respect for religious teachers in that time and place, reserved. Nicodemus approaches Jesus not as an enemy but as an inquisitive student who genuinely wants to learn something that he does not know. Moreover, he acknowledges Jesus as a miracle worker: "No one can do these signs that you do apart from the presence of God" (v. 2). As an aside, we might also connect personally with the inquisitive Nicodemus's words for they betray the fact that Nicodemus seems to consider Jesus as just one more prophet. Nicodemus is not a bad man. He is a highly thought of enquiring minded man of good character.

Conversation
Like everything else in scripture, this conversation is recorded for our benefit. As witnesses to the heart-to-heart exchange that ensues we have an opportunity to learn as much as Nicodemus about what truly matters. What is intriguing is that Jesus essentially disregards Nicodemus' compliments and platitudes. Nor does the Lord take time to discuss whatever societal or religious relationships Nicodemus might have. Instead, the master turns his attention to the man's heart. In his own way, Jesus lets Nicodemus know that his religion, no matter how Jewish, how historic, or how widely followed, always comes up short. "Very truly, I tell you, no one can see the kingdom of God without being born from above" (v. 3). Christ's metaphor is so commonly understood that even young children can connect with it. We all came into the world through birth and rare is there one among us who has not marveled at the birth of a new baby. Jesus relates to birth but it is birth with a difference. The birth of which Jesus speaks is immediately elevated above the norm. This is no ordinary birth. It is birth "from above."

Nicodemus recognizes the difference right away and responds with a question: "How can anyone be born after having grown old? Can one enter a second time into the mother's womb and be born?" (v. 4). In his response, the Lord expands his birth metaphor: "Very truly, I tell you, no one can enter the kingdom of God without being born of water and Spirit. What is born of the flesh is flesh, and what is born of the Spirit is spirit. Do not be astonished that I said to you,

'You must be born from above.' The wind blows where it chooses, and you hear the sound of it, but you do not know where it comes from or where it goes. So it is with everyone who is born of the Spirit" (vv. 5-8).

Water birth the learned Nicodemus could understand. Even though each of them had entered the world through water birth, the Pharisees regard it as unclean. Spiritual birth, however, is beyond anything he would have studied in the school of the Pharisees. They are much too set in their ways to be open to anything like that. Moreover, when Jesus introduces the subject of the wind, Nicodemus knows that no one could consistently and accurately predict the weather because the wind has a quality about it that is quite unpredictable. In fact, we know this is true even today for our best experts still miss it with their weather forecasts. Not only that, but now Jesus introduces a divine imperative in his words, "You must be born from above." To Nicodemus it sounds as if there are no other options and we can imagine that if Nicodemus was inquisitive before, now he must be completely intrigued. "How can these things be?" he probes Jesus for an answer.

For that moment, at least, it seems Nicodemus does not remember Ezekiel's apocalyptic vision of the valley of dry bones that pictures the manner in which Yahweh would restore his people. The wind of God would move across that which was already dead and it would become alive. Ezekiel received the Lord's call,

Prophesy to these bones, and say to them: O dry bones, hear the word of the Lord. Thus says the Lord God to these bones: I will cause breath to enter you, and you shall live. I will lay sinews on you, and will cause flesh to come upon you, and cover you with skin, and put breath in you, and you shall live; and you shall know that I am the Lord.
(Ezekiel 37:4-6)

The record testifies that when the wind of God moved over those dead bones they came alive. Ezekiel saw it happen. Then God spoke to him again,

> Therefore prophesy, and say to them, Thus says the Lord God: "I am going to open your graves, and bring you up from your graves, O my people; and I will bring you back to the land of Israel. And you shall know that I am the Lord, when I open your graves, and bring you up from your graves, O my people. I will put my spirit within you, and you shall live, and I will place you on your own soil; then you shall know that I, the Lord, have spoken and will act," says the Lord.
> (Ezekiel 37:12-14)

This is what happens every time the wind of God — the Holy Spirit — moves across the cold dead heart of a lost sinner, and when the sinner comes alive by faith in God's Son, Jesus Christ, what once was dead comes to life. That is why Jesus calls it being born again from above. That new birth is bigger than church membership alone. It is bigger than social programs alone. It cannot be received through genetics from those who lived before us. It must happen anew for every one of us in each new generation. Hence Jesus says to this religious leader, Nicodemus, "You must be born from above" (John 3:7). A religious scholar he may have been, but in the eyes of Jesus, Nicodemus is still living in spiritual darkness. Perhaps he reminds you of someone you know. Maybe he reminds you of yourself. Perhaps Jesus is speaking to your heart just now and saying, "You must be born from above." If this is the case, how will you respond? Will you continue to lie in dry bones valley? Or will you breathe deeply of God's wind and rise up in newness of life?

In case Nicodemus does not connect with that vision, Jesus reaches back once more into Israel's history. He brings before Nicodemus a memory of the time when Israel was tramping through the wilderness, complaining and whining against God and against Moses. They were all caught up in how tough their life was now. Some of them actually said they preferred slavery in Egypt. We read that it was then God sent poisonous snakes among the people. The snakes bit the Israelites and many of them died. After Moses petitioned God on their behalf, God told Moses to make a poisonous serpent, set it up on a pole, and all who were bitten would look at it and live. Scripture says, "Moses made a serpent of bronze, and put it upon a pole; and whenever a serpent bit someone, that person would look at the serpent of bronze and live" (Numbers 21:9).

Now Jesus tells Nicodemus, "Just as Moses lifted up the serpent in the wilderness, so must the Son of Man be lifted up, that whoever believes in him may have eternal life" (John 3:15).

The conversation now turns to the reason for all that has happened to this point. If you grew up in the church, attended Sunday school — or maybe even if you did not — you likely have heard what comes next. In one simple sentence that many Christians have memorized, Jesus states the purpose for everything that he has told Nicodemus until now and, more than that, the reason why he, Jesus, is here on earth. It is the gospel in a nutshell, a jiffy for eternity: "For God so loved the world that he gave his only Son, so that everyone who believes in him may not perish but may have eternal life" (John 3:16). It is short but not shallow.

Perhaps no version translates this eternally powerful sentence any better than the old King James Version, in which many of us learned and memorized it for the first time: "For God so loved the world, that he gave his only begotten Son, that whosoever believeth in him should not perish, but have everlasting life" (John 3:16 KJV).

Commitment

God's passionate love commitment to this world he created and whose people chose to walk away from him is so great that he sent his own Son to earth with the express mission of bringing new breath to spiritually dead people. Jesus puts his mission this way in Luke's gospel, "The Son of Man came to seek out and to save the lost" (Luke 19:10). The gospel is ultimately given in a short simple message each time. It is not complicated. Even a child can understand it. What is it telling us?

First, it tells us that God wants us to experience true love and not human love, which often is self-serving and impure in its motivation. Human love is almost always small in its thinking. It usually is given on the basis of what the lover wants in return. God's love is different. It is, in fact, so different, so much bigger, that it takes a special Greek word to describe it. That word is *agapao*. Human love may be motivated by self-centered desire and say, "I love you for what I can take from you." The implied message is "when I receive from you what I want, my love may well dissipate like the morning fog." Or human love may be motivated by hope of mutuality and say, "I love you so long as you love me back." God's love is a world apart from either of those loves. It is motivated by God's desire to love us because "God is love" (1 John 4:16). God's love says, "I love you simply because I love you." The truth is that we possess nothing and control nothing that God needs. Nor can we ever hope to extend to God a mutual brotherly love. The only thing we need to do to know God's love is receive it.

This jiffy sentence that speaks to us of eternity also speaks to the span of God's love. It tells us that "God so loved the world." The word "so" now gets our focus. We can picture a child stretching out her arms as wide as she can and saying to a parent, "I love you this big." The parent in turn

37

stretches out her arms, which stretch even wider, and says, "And I love you bigger." The span of God's love is wider and longer and deeper than any human arms can ever stretch, than any human heart can ever love, and any human love can ever go. This sentence that takes only a jiffy to read takes an eternity to fully comprehend. It is short but not shallow!

For a Pharisee, the notion that God's love extended beyond the Jewish race into the whole world turned his whole theological system of belief upside down. The Pharisees were lover-less. For the first time in his life Nicodemus was being confronted with a theology of love that demolished all the fences his sect had taught him throughout his life.

A wonderful old Christian song "The Love Of God Is Greater Far" describes this love well:

> The love of God is greater far
> Than tongue or pen can ever tell.
> It goes beyond the highest star
> And reaches to the lowest hell.
> The guilty pair, bowed down with care,
> God gave His Son to win;
> His erring child He reconciled,
> And pardoned from his sin.
>
> O love of God, how rich and pure!
> How measureless and strong!
> It shall forevermore endure
> The saints' and angels' song.
>
> When hoary time shall pass away,
> And earthly thrones and kingdoms fall;
> When men who here refuse to pray,
> On rocks and hills and mountains call;
> God's love, so sure, shall still endure,
> All measureless and strong;
> Redeeming grace to Adam's race —
> The saints' and angels' song.

Could we with ink the ocean fill,
And were the skies of parchment made;
Were every stalk on earth a quill,
And every man a scribe by trade;
To write the love of God above
Would drain the ocean dry;
Nor could the scroll contain the whole,
Though stretched from sky to sky.[1]

Perhaps one thing that makes this old song especially fascinating is that its third verse was penned not by the song's original author, Pastor Frederick Lehman, but penciled on a cell wall by a man who was consigned to live in an asylum because he was adjudged to be mentally troubled beyond hope. His lines were discovered when hospital personnel entered his cubicle room to place his body on a gurney to take it to the mortuary after he died. Even there God's love reached him! There simply is no place that God's love cannot be found.

The message of the song is first that God's love is immeasurable and second, God's love is inescapable. "God *so* loved" tells us about the span of God's love.

Another measure of love is what love is willing to do for its object. Here we read, "For God so loved the world that he gave his only Son, so that everyone who believes in him may not perish but may have eternal life."

Here is a cow-eyed fellow who telephones his girlfriend and tells her that there is nothing he would not do for her. "Why, I would swim in a sea of sharks or jump into a den of hungry wild lions just to prove how much I love you, my one and only sweetheart!" he exclaims. Then he adds, "And if my buddies don't want to go to tonight's baseball game I will come by and get you so that I don't have to sit alone on the bleachers!"

"God so loved that he gave his only Son." This love of his is not only beyond all limits. It is willing to do whatever it takes to redeem its beloved. The death of Jesus on a rough-hewn Roman cross is the all-time ultimate demonstration of how far God's love is willing to go.

On December 14, 2012, America was stunned when the news broke about twenty-year-old Adam Lanza, entering the Sandy Hook Elementary School in Newtown, Connecticut, and shooting twenty children and six adult staff members. Earlier that morning, Adam Lanza had slaughtered his own mother. Americans heard news reports of mass shootings before in high schools, movie theaters, and houses of worship. What grabbed the nation's heart in a new and deeper way than in any previous mass killing incident was that most of the fatalities were first-grade children. What would you do to defend your child from that kind of cruel death? Would you not respond that you would do whatever would be necessary, including sacrificing your own life?

God is different. God not only allowed his Son to be cruelly and brutally killed, he sent his only Son to die for us. He who knows our worst, loves us best of all. Such is God's amazing love! It was not that God did not love his Son. Scripture tells us that God loved and was proud of his Son. John writes, "The Father loves the Son and shows him all that he himself is doing" (John 5:20). Matthew records a highlight moment when Jesus was baptized: "A voice from heaven said, 'This is my Son, the Beloved, with whom I am well pleased' " (Matthew 3:17). God loved his Son and was pleased with him; yet God sent his Son to die for us. That is amazing love!

The most powerful demonstration of true love this world will ever see happened one Friday afternoon at calvary when a cross was erected and on that cross God demonstrated that he loved us even more than his Son! That was a love beyond amazing!

There is a word about life in this sentence: "God so loved the world that he gave his only Son, so that everyone who believes in him may not perish but may have eternal life." It speaks about the value that God, in his grace, places on each of our lives. He considers us of more value than his only Son. Such is the value of our lives to God who made us. "Indeed, God did not send the Son into the world to condemn the world, but in order that the world might be saved through him" (v. 17).

Did you hear that sentence? Despite what many of us may have heard or feared, this God who comes to us in Jesus is for us. He is not motivated to condemn but to save us. For Nicodemus the Pharisee this was a new vision of God. All his pharisaical training to this moment had been directed toward making him a judge of other people but now he meets the God of no condemnation. No wonder he was motivated to challenge his fellow Pharisees with those words, "Our law does not judge people without first giving them a hearing to find out what they are doing, does it?" (John 7:51). Meeting this God who comes to us in Christ has a way of changing everything about how we view all of life. To God be the glory!

Nicodemus' questions found answers in God's love in Jesus Christ and ours do too. In a jiffy, Nicodemus' life was changed for eternity. If you belong to Jesus, whether you received Christ suddenly or over a period of time, your life was changed by the self-same truth for the same eternity and you will one day be in heaven with Nicodemus and, far more important, with the Lord of all good love, Christ Jesus.

Nicodemus had his questions and his answers. Now I have a question for you to answer: How will you respond to such an amazing love as this? The only reasonable response is to receive this love and vow that you will spend your life living out what it means to be one of God's greatly beloved children. Do you have a better answer?

1. Frederick M. Lehman, *The Love of God* (1917), public domain.

Lent 3
John 4:5-42

The Womb of Amazing Grace!

So he came to a Samaritan city called Sychar, near the plot of ground that Jacob had given to his son Joseph. Jacob's well was there, and Jesus, tired out by his journey, was sitting by the well. It was about noon. A Samaritan woman came to draw water, and Jesus said to her, "Give me a drink." (His disciples had gone to the city to buy food.) The Samaritan woman said to him, "How is it that you, a Jew, ask a drink of me, a woman of Samaria?" (Jews do not share things in common with Samaritans.) Jesus answered her, "If you knew the gift of God, and who it is that is saying to you, 'Give me a drink,' you would have asked him, and he would have given you living water." The woman said to him, "Sir, you have no bucket, and the well is deep. Where do you get that living water? Are you greater than our ancestor Jacob, who gave us the well, and with his sons and his flocks drank from it?" Jesus said to her, "Everyone who drinks of this water will be thirsty again, but those who drink of the water that I will give them will never be thirsty. The water that I will give will become in them a spring of water gushing up to eternal life." The woman said to him, "Sir, give me this water, so that I may never be thirsty or have to keep coming here to draw water." Jesus said to her, "Go, call your husband, and come back." The woman answered him, "I have no husband." Jesus said to her, "You are right in saying, 'I have no husband'; for you have had five husbands, and the one you have now is not your husband. What you have said is true!" The woman said to him, "Sir, I see that you are a prophet. Our ancestors worshiped on this mountain, but you say that the place where people must worship is in Jerusalem." Jesus said to her, "Woman, believe me, the hour is coming when you will worship the Father neither on this mountain nor in Jerusalem. You worship what you do not know; we worship what we know, for salvation is from the Jews. But the hour is coming, and is now here, when the true worshipers will worship the Father in spirit and truth, for the Father seeks such as these to worship him. God is spirit, and those who worship him must worship in spirit and truth." The woman said to him, "I know that Messiah is coming" (who is called Christ). "When he comes, he will proclaim all things to us." Jesus said to her, "I am he, the one who is speaking to you." Just then his disciples came. They were astonished that he was speaking with a woman, but no one said, "What do you want?" or, "Why are you speaking with her?" Then the woman left her water jar and went back to the city. She said to the people, "Come and see a man who told me everything I have ever done! He cannot be the Messiah, can he?" They left the city and were on their way to him. Meanwhile the disciples were urging him, "Rabbi, eat something." But he said to them, "I have food to eat that you do not know about." So the disciples said to one another, "Surely no one has brought him something to eat?" Jesus said to them, "My food is to do the will of him who sent me and to complete his work. Do you not say, 'Four months more, then comes the harvest'? But I tell you, look around you, and see how the fields are ripe for harvesting. The reaper is already receiving wages and is gathering fruit for eternal life, so that sower and reaper may rejoice together. For here the saying holds true, 'One sows and another reaps.' I sent you to reap that for which you did not labor. Others have labored, and you have entered into their labor." Many Samaritans from that city believed in him because of the woman's testimony, "He told me everything I have ever done." So when the Samaritans came to him, they asked him to stay with them; and he stayed there two days. And many more believed because of his word. They said to the woman, "It is no longer because of what you said that we believe, for we have heard for ourselves, and we know that this is truly the Savior of the world."

In John 3 we have the record of an amazing encounter between Jesus and Nicodemus, a man described as a leader among the Jews and a member of the sect of the Pharisees. John 4 presents another stunning encounter, one even more startling. It involves a person from "the other side of the religious and political tracks," someone who lived out her life at the other end of the social and religious strata of that time and place. It is hard to imagine any greater contrast than that which is pictured in these two chapters. Philosophically, theologically, and politically a world of difference existed between Nicodemus the Pharisee and this woman of Samaria. Talk about Mars and Venus! No self-respecting Pharisee would have been caught dead in this Samaritan woman's company. Pharisees considered this woman and all residents of Samaria unworthy prospects for their religion. Think about the contrast presented between Nicodemus in John 3 and this woman in John 4. She was, as has been emphasized already, a Samaritan. Moreover, she was not just a Samaritan, but also a woman. On top of that, she was a woman with a deeply scarred past. So, it is fair to say that to the Pharisees' way of thinking, she had three strikes against her and was unworthy of redemption of any kind. Given her history and current lifestyle, the law of the Pharisees had one response for her if she ever was caught in Jerusalem: Stone her to death!

Jesus looks at her situation from an entirely different perspective. He sees in her something worth saving. He turns a momentary encounter by a well into the womb of amazing grace. For the Pharisees, it was an unthinkable idea. For us, this moment has demonstrated for 2,000 years just how far beyond our imaginations God's grace is prepared to go to give new birth to a lost soul. Nobody was more hated by the Pharisees than the Samaritans. Most Jews would walk miles out of their way rather than go through Samaria. Jesus, however, "came to a Samaritan city called Sychar" (v. 4). Actually, the Greek text indicates that Jesus had to go there because he was driven by godly compulsion to go into the area others feared and avoided.

The hatred between the Jews and the Samaritans was a two-way street. The Pharisees hated the Samaritans, and the Samaritans carried an equally intense vitriol for the Pharisees. The Samaritans were an ethno-religious group whose religion was based on their Samaritan Torah. That Torah claimed the worship of the Samaritans to be the one true religion of the ancient Israelites prior to the Babyonian exile. Their religious leaders taught that it was preserved by those who remained in the land of Israel. For them, Judaism, the religion of the Pharisees, was a related but altered and amended religion that had been brought back by those returning from exile. You can see right away why the Pharisees held that theology in contempt. Furthermore, for the Pharisees over time the name Samaritan had become a derogatory, racially motivated term that was applied with a broad brush to all the inhabitants of Israel's northern kingdom and their progeny.

According to 1 Kings 16:24, the Samaritans inhabited a hill that the wicked King Omri once purchased to establish a new capital for the northern kingdom of Israel, an attempt to one day supplant Jerusalem as the national capital. As one generation gave way to another, these northern kingdom Jews often intermarried with people from other tribes thus diluting the bloodline. This also was contemptible to the Pharisees for it diluted the pure Jewish bloodstream. Having married outside their own race, the Samaritans, as we might expect, produced children, who were seen by the Pharisees as children of mixed heritage and thus children of a lesser god or gods. As time passed, the name Samaritan gradually evolved into a kind of slur, a word used to speak of people of questionable pedigree. To say merely that they were the unwelcome country cousins among the proud southern kingdom Jews would be an understatement. Add to this their location to Samaria's more relaxed religious environment those southern kingdom Jewish mischief-makers, agitators, renegades, and rogues who grew weary of the strict interpretation of Jewish laws in Jerusalem and moved to the *laissez-faire* environment they found in Samaria. The Samaritans knew well of the southern kingdom citizens' intolerance for them and, when it suited their purposes, aggravated the Jews by reminding anyone who would listen that they were, in fact, cousins and other children of Abraham. All in all, for southern kingdom Jews, Samaritans were the kind of relatives you wish would just not tell anybody that you are somehow related!

Of all the personal encounters involving Jesus, this one with the Samaritan woman is surely the most remarkable for it put real live skin on the notion that God's love extended beyond the Jews and into the whole world. Yes, even to the Samaritans! This Samaritan woman recognized something different about this right away, "How is it that you, a Jew, ask a drink of me, a woman of Samaria?" (John 4:9). She had difficulty absorbing the idea that this Jewish man who spoke for God would step across the long-established social and religious fences erected in the minds of people on both sides of this divide.

So here he is a sinless Savior meeting a woman whose life is, in some ways, a perfect demonstration of sin and its devastating effects on a life. That she comes out for water in the noontime heat tells us something about her. Historians record that the well was the early morning and late afternoon gathering place where women of that region came together to fetch water for the day and to catch up on the news. Some would call that gossip. This woman clearly is not a part of that gossip gathering, but we can imagine that she had been in the past — perhaps still is — the topic of those gossip sessions. She comes to fetch water at noon because it is not likely anyone else would be there, and she could avoid the whispers and stares of the women who come early in the day. She is an outcast even among her own people. Yet to Jesus, she is a woman in need of God's amazing grace.

Here, for us, is a lesson in how we might be used to lead other people to faith in Jesus. "I tell you, look around you, and see how the fields are ripe for harvesting" (John 4:35).

Sowing and Reaping

The first lesson we receive from Jesus is that when it comes to leading unbelievers to faith there is a process that is not unlike the laws of the harvest. "For here the saying holds true, 'One sows and another reaps' " (John 4:37). If you have ever sown a garden, you already know that sowing requires preparing the soil and planting seeds. It is an operation that takes time and teaching. Every good gardener will tell you that she had a teacher, someone who took the time to show her how to do what was necessary for the best results.

Similarly, when it comes to preparing for God's kingdom harvest, bringing people to faith in God through Jesus does not usually happen in an instant. Hearts and minds must be prepared to receive the seed of the gospel through time, teaching, demonstration, and influence. The truth is that this often takes place without any noticeable outcome. Being a gospel-seed sower calls for patience and consistency on the part of the one sowing.

A little boy watched his daddy carefully sow some seeds and set up some runners for peas to grow. Three days later, the little boy was playing outside when that experience came to his mind and he decided that he would check on what was happening. When he returned to the place where his daddy had sowed just three days before, it seemed to him that nothing had changed. He decided that he should check to see if something might be wrong below the soil. He found a stick and began to dig some holes in the soil. Fortunately for him, he had not been doing that too long when his dad came to check on his garden and caught the youngster digging. "Son, what on earth are you doing?" the dad asked. "I'm checking to see why we don't have any peas yet," the lad replied. The dad had to exercise some restraint, which he did as he patiently began to instruct his little boy that some things, such as growing a garden can take time and one has to do the work then leave it alone for God to go to work.

That is exactly what happens when we set about leading someone to faith in Jesus! To the best of our ability we can prepare the heart and sow the gospel seed but nothing will happen until God goes to work. It all takes time. The prophet Jeremiah prophesied for almost half a century with little sign of success. Some people would look at Jeremiah's life and say it was a waste of time and effort, but God does not measure success as we might. He measures success by faithfulness.

A good gardener will tell you that reaping a harvest that has been sown is a process. The same is true in our witnessing. It usually involves people hearing God's word and deciding to heed it. When conversion comes, it comes about with wonderful joy and excitement about the results. Here, however, is a truth worth retaining: The sowing and the reaping may not be witnessed and accomplished by the same person. "Here the saying holds true, 'One sows and another reaps.' I sent you to reap that for which you did not labor. Others have labored, and you have entered into their labor" (John 4:37-38). There can be a long time between the sowing and the reaping when it comes to bringing a gospel harvest home. It does not always happen on the same watch.

Reaping a Harvest We Did Not Sow

Here is another point well worth heeding: We may reap where others have sown. "I sent you to reap that for which you did not labor. Others have labored, and you have entered into their labor" (John 4:38). In Samaria it was Jesus who plants the first seed when he tells the woman at the well about his eternally quenching water. She, in turn, goes out telling what she had heard from him to everyone who would listen. We read, "The woman left her water jar and went back to the city. She said to the people, 'Come and see a man who told me everything I have ever done! He cannot be the Messiah, can he?' They left the city and were on their way to him" (John 4:28-30). The disciples would reap a harvest of human souls they had not sown. This is the biblical pattern for the Bible teaches us that "salvation belongs to the LORD" (Jonah 2:9 ESV). That is to say that when it comes to saving souls, God must always have first done his part in what happens.

So it is when we find someone who seems ready to obey the call of Jesus to come and follow. There is a great likelihood that someone else did some sowing ahead of us. It might have been a parent, grandparent, sibling, friend, teacher, or pastor. What matters is that God was present to authenticate what human sowers and reapers had a hand in doing. The apostle Paul says it like this,

> I planted, Apollos watered, but God gave the growth. So neither the one who plants nor the one who waters is anything, but only God who gives the growth. The one who plants and the one who waters have a common purpose, and each will receive wages according to the labor of each. For we are God's servants, working together.
> (1 Corinthians 3:6-9)

It is dangerous when we persuade ourselves that we won someone to Christ all by ourselves. We can and should rejoice when a life is changed by the gospel but we must never forget that God is necessary in every conversion. Jesus says, "I am the vine; you are the branches. Whoever abides in me and I in him, he it is that bears much fruit, for apart from me you can do nothing" (John 15:5 ESV).

A Call to Persistence in Sowing and Reaping

Someone, somewhere, or, in all likelihood, a series of "someones" sowed the seeds that produced the new birth in your life. If you are a believer you have passed through the womb of amazing grace for no one gets saved alone. Indeed, this gospel, given to us through those people through

God's amazing grace, is designed to always exist just one generation from extinction. Heresies cannot kill the church. There have always been heresies and the church has always overcome them. Despots cannot destroy the church for there have always been tyrants and dictators — Herod Agrippa, Adolf Hitler, Idi Amin, Nicolae Ceauescu — whose goal was to stamp out the gospel flame. None has ever succeeded and none ever will. In fact, history records that the actions of such people have served to make the church stronger. Having said this, killing the church is not impossible. To kill the church or to annihilate the influence of the gospel on our world is really not a hard thing, because all that it takes is for our generation of Christians to stop telling God's story and doing God's work. In a similar way, if a farmer wants his farmland to grow over in weeds and stubble, all he needs to do is not sow for one season. We are called to bear witness for Jesus' sake. His last great command — we call it the Great Commission — was "go therefore and make disciples of all nations, baptizing them in the name of the Father and of the Son and of the Holy Spirit, and teaching them to obey everything that I have commanded you. And remember, I am with you always, to the end of the age" (Matthew 28:19-20). It is a call for all his disciples and for all time.

Sometimes we sow the seeds that fulfill this command through our example. Peter writes that an ungodly husband may be won over by the life example of a godly wife: "Even if some of them do not obey the word, they may be won over without a word by their wives' conduct, when they see the purity and reverence of your lives" (1 Peter 3:1-2). As it was with Jeremiah, so it may be with us. Successful disciple-making often calls for patience, commitment, and stick-to-it-iveness.

We can take comfort in God's assurance that spreading God's word is never futile. God himself assures us,

> For as the rain and the snow come down from heaven, and do not return there until they have watered the earth, making it bring forth and sprout, giving seed to the sower and bread to the eater, so shall my word be that goes out from my mouth; it shall not return to me empty, but it shall accomplish that which I purpose, and succeed in the thing for which I sent it.
> (Isaiah 55:10-11)

We are not responsible for reaping the harvest but we are responsible for planting the seeds of harvest. Again God himself says,

> I have made you a sentinel for the house of Israel; whenever you hear a word from my mouth, you shall give them warning from me. If I say to the wicked, "You shall surely die," and you give them no warning, or speak to warn the wicked from their wicked way, in order to save their life, those wicked persons shall die for their iniquity; but their blood I will require at your hand. But if you warn the wicked, and they do not turn from their wickedness, or from their wicked way, they shall die for their iniquity; but you will have saved your life.
> (Ezekiel 3:17-19)

Although we may never reap a harvest from our sowing, we can be thankful that our efforts on God's behalf are never unnoticed by him.

When we witness for Jesus we do so in the power of God's providence. The story is told of a group of men who came together in a lakeside community to form a new club. Because of their location and the stories of great fish being caught in the lake, they decided to call themselves "The Fishing Club." Someone said he heard that the lake fish were hungry. So week after week, month after month, and year after year, the members of The Fishing Club came together. In their meetings they would always discuss what was being caught in the lake. They brought in guest experts to tell them how they should catch one kind of fish or another. Other experts advised them about bait and tackle. They were always on the lookout for new and better ways to catch fish. They sponsored special drives to gain new members who were invited to come and join them in their meetings. They even built a fantastic new building right on the edge of the lake and they erected a sign on it that said "The Fishing Club Headquarters." So they kept on meeting, learning, and talking. There was just one thing they never did however: They did not fish!

Imagine how insulted their collective ego was when one day a stranger came to that community and suggested that people who do not go out on the lake determined to catch some fish are really not fishermen at all. They gave the stranger a tour of The Fishermen's Club Headquarters building. They talked about rods and reels and bait and fishing schedules. The stranger was impressed by their collective knowledge on the subject of fishing. Yet when they finished showing him around and impressing him with their knowledge he responded, "This is all very impressive and you are all very nice fellows, but the truth is still that men who don't go fishing, people who only talk about it, will never catch a fish, and therefore do not deserve to be called fishermen."

Wouldn't you agree?

Now, let me bring this little parable closer to home: Once upon a time there was a group of people who decided to form a church. At their first meeting they agreed that they needed more members and that the only way to get them would be through a determined program of evangelism. They discussed the subject and brought in experts and read books and… I think you are beginning to get the point.

The question is, what are you going to do about it? When are you going to start? If not now, when? If not you, who? Evangelism, bringing people to Jesus, is the call of every church member. Just what will you do about it? As far as you are concerned, will it be acceptable for this church to die in this generation?

Jesus says, "Follow me, and I will make you fishers of people" (Matthew 4:19).

Let's go out this week and bait some hooks!

Lent 4
John 9:1-41

Here's Mud in Your Eye!

As he walked along, he saw a man blind from birth. His disciples asked him, "Rabbi, who sinned, this man or his parents, that he was born blind?" Jesus answered, "Neither this man nor his parents sinned; he was born blind so that God's works might be revealed in him. We must work the works of him who sent me while it is day; night is coming when no one can work. As long as I am in the world, I am the light of the world." When he had said this, he spat on the ground and made mud with the saliva and spread the mud on the man's eyes, saying to him, "Go, wash in the pool of Siloam" (which means Sent). Then he went and washed and came back able to see. The neighbors and those who had seen him before as a beggar began to ask, "Is this not the man who used to sit and beg?" Some were saying, "It is he." Others were saying, "No, but it is someone like him." He kept saying, "I am the man." But they kept asking him, "Then how were your eyes opened?" He answered, "The man called Jesus made mud, spread it on my eyes, and said to me, 'Go to Siloam and wash.' Then I went and washed and received my sight." They said to him, "Where is he?" He said, "I do not know." They brought to the Pharisees the man who had formerly been blind. Now it was a Sabbath day when Jesus made the mud and opened his eyes. Then the Pharisees also began to ask him how he had received his sight. He said to them, "He put mud on my eyes. Then I washed, and now I see." Some of the Pharisees said, "This man is not from God, for he does not observe the Sabbath." But others said, "How can a man who is a sinner perform such signs?" And they were divided. So they said again to the blind man, "What do you say about him? It was your eyes he opened." He said, "He is a prophet." The Jews did not believe that he had been blind and had received his sight until they called the parents of the man who had received his sight and asked them, "Is this your son, who you say was born blind? How then does he now see?" His parents answered, "We know that this is our son, and that he was born blind; but we do not know how it is that now he sees, nor do we know who opened his eyes. Ask him; he is of age. He will speak for himself." His parents said this because they were afraid of the Jews; for the Jews had already agreed that anyone who confessed Jesus to be the Messiah would be put out of the synagogue. Therefore his parents said, "He is of age; ask him." So for the second time they called the man who had been blind, and they said to him, "Give glory to God! We know that this man is a sinner." He answered, "I do not know whether he is a sinner. One thing I do know, that though I was blind, now I see." They said to him, "What did he do to you? How did he open your eyes?" He answered them, "I have told you already, and you would not listen. Why do you want to hear it again? Do you also want to become his disciples?" Then they reviled him, saying, "You are his disciple, but we are disciples of Moses. We know that God has spoken to Moses, but as for this man, we do not know where he comes from." The man answered, "Here is an astonishing thing! You do not know where he comes from, and yet he opened my eyes. We know that God does not listen to sinners, but he does listen to one who worships him and obeys his will. Never since the world began has it been heard that anyone opened the eyes of a person born blind. If this man were not from God, he could do nothing." They answered him, "You were born entirely in sins, and are you trying to teach us?" And they drove him out. Jesus heard that they had driven him out, and when he found him, he said, "Do you believe in the Son of Man?" He answered, "And who is he, sir? Tell me, so that I may believe in him." Jesus said to him, "You have seen him, and the one speaking with you is he." He said, "Lord, I believe." And he worshiped him. Jesus said, "I came into this world for judgment so that those who do not see may see, and those who do see may become blind." Some of the Pharisees near him heard this and said to him, "Surely we are not blind, are we?" Jesus said to them, "If you were blind, you would not have sin. But now that you say, 'We see,' your sin remains."

"Just the facts, ma'am!" That phrase, often attributed to Sergeant Joe Friday of *Dragnet* fame, even though it did not originate with him, goes straight to the point. Now here is another "just the facts personality": Julius Caesar was admired for his ability to make uncluttered summations of his great achievements. In a few words Caesar could lay bare the story of his accomplishments. Perhaps none of his statements is any better known than that famous terse tricolon that has followed Caesar since his quick four-hour defeat of Pharnaces II of Pontus in the city of Zela (currently Zile in modern Turkey) since April 47 BC. Impressed with his performance as a warrior, Caesar informed the Roman Senate using just three Latin verbs: *Veni, vidi, vici* meaning: "I came. I saw. I conquered!"

As impressive as Caesar's victory was to his own already over-inflated ego, it does not hold a candle to the testimony of this young man healed by Jesus: "One thing I do know, that though I was blind, now I see" (v. 25), explains this man who had never seen daylight before and who became in an instant the subject of the most exciting miracle in the gospels. From that day forward that young man could no more be silenced than a bird can cease singing its song. His is the most fascinating reaction of the five miracles recorded in the chapter.

Helen Keller was asked on one occasion whether being blind was the worst affliction in the world. She smiled, "No. Not half so bad as having two good eyes and seeing nothing!" In the account of this miracle, there are many characters who have two physically good eyes yet they are spiritually blind.

Blinded By a Quest for Someone to Blame
The disciples, looking for a simple answer to a complicated situation, do not see the blind man as one in need of ministry but as a topic for theological debate. They are blind to what is really happening in this moment between the young man and Jesus. They ask Jesus, "Rabbi, who sinned, this man or his parents, that he was born blind?" (v. 2). Their

question is typical because it was rooted in the logic of their world and, indeed, our world. The common Jewish belief was that suffering and affliction are always the fruit of some great sin. "Whom should we blame?" they wanted to know.

With 24 good eyes they could not see! Like inquisitive three year olds, they want to know, "Why? Why? Why?" "Why is he like this? Was it something he did or something his parents did?" They want simple answers to all of life's questions. They want, as we often do, a rule book of neatly packaged theology to answer all of their "why" questions. That, however, is not the way of life on this earth. The disciples, as close as they live to Jesus, do not realize that since the fall of Adam in Eden's Garden everything about this world has been confused and complicated.

Neither of the possibilities the disciples put forward have merit. They had yet to learn that it is wrong to conclude there is always a clear cause and effect for every instance of human suffering and depravity. It is also wrong to assume that God permits every instance of human suffering because he intends to perform a miracle. Jesus is speaking about this man's circumstances. In doing so, he does not reveal all the reasons why the man was born blind. The disciples see his condition as evidence of God's judgment. Jesus sees it as an opportunity for God's grace.

We need to remember that we will not always understand why little babies are born with cleft palettes and lips, or Spina bifida, or other handicaps, including blindness, and God alone can turn those deformities and handicaps into something that will bring good to the people and glory to God's name.

Charles Riley (not his real name) was born with Down syndrome in a small southern town where medical care was limited. Charles's mother, well into life's middle years when Charles was born, was a godly woman. His father spent years wrestling unsuccessfully with alcoholism and had a reputation as the town drunk, who drank his business out of existence and could not hold a job. The couple already had two children and had not planned on having a third. Not long after Charles was born his father committed suicide, leaving his wife to raise all three children. Gloria Riley had not worked in some years but was able to keep things together through the years of her husband's drunkenness because of a modest inheritance and whatever occasional income her husband was able to earn. It was a situation made for tragedy upon tragedy. Gloria returned to teaching school, leaving her three children under the care of good neighbors and friends.

As time passed and Charles grew older, he began to walk around the community speaking to anyone who would give him the time of day. In those days that little town was divided between blacks and whites and old timers and a few newcomers. Charles never seemed to recognize those differences, and his daily walkabouts, friendly demeanor, and winsome personality was well received by everyone. As the years went by, Charles became the rallying point around which people of various backgrounds and interests set aside their differences and came together. God used that young man as his instrument to overcome community divisions. When Charles finally died at the age of 37, the whole community gathered to remember him. The healing touch he brought continues to this day. When he was a youngster bearing all the marks of Down syndrome, some people saw him as a deformed person born into some of the worst imaginable circumstances. God saw him as his peacemaker, having already said, "Blessed are the peacemakers, for they will be called children of God" (Matthew 5:9).

There are some things we do not fully understand. Jesus reminds the disciples, "Neither this man nor his parents sinned; he was born blind so that God's works might be revealed in him. We must work the works of him who sent me while it is day; night is coming when no one can work" (vv.

3-4). The blind man's new sight shows that Jesus, the "light of the world," can dispel darkness in unique ways. Could it have been that his reason for spitting on the ground was not only to redeem the mud but also to allow that blind man to hear what the Lord was about. We do know that Mark's gospel records Jesus used his saliva applied to the tongue to heal a deaf man with a speech impediment in Decapolis and to the eyes of another blind man near Bethsaida (Mark 7:33; Mark 8:23).

In our sophisticated age, we may think these healing methods crude but consider another possibility: Could it have been that Jesus was demonstrating God's ability to use even that which is dirty to demonstrate God's power to accomplish a pure cure? This we know from the record: sight was restored by clay that was made by him whose breath had once breathed life into a man made of clay.

Blinded by Low Expectations
Filled with a strange new hope they came,
The blind, the leper, the sick, the lame.
Frail of body and spent of soul…
As many as touched Him were made whole.

On every tongue was the Healer's name,
Through all the land they spread His fame.
But doubt clung tight to its old wooden crutch
Saying, "We must not expect too much."

Down through the ages a promise came,
Healing for sorrow and sin and shame,
Help for the helpless and caught in life's grind,
Healing for the body and soul and mind.

The Christ we follow is still the same,
With blessings that all who will may claim.
But how often we miss Love's healing touch,
By thinking, "We must not expect too much."
— Author unknown

What do you think? Can we miss out on the healing power of Christ simply because we're afraid to expect too much? Do you believe that Jesus Christ still has the power to heal a broken body, a broken heart, a broken dream, a broken relationship? Do you need Christ's healing touch for your bitterness, depression, grief, or fear? Do you need to be healed of cynicism? Do you need to know his power to overcome sin, lust, or addictions?

Hear these words again through the ears of your heart:

The Christ we follow is still the same,
With blessings that all who will may claim.
But how often we miss Love's healing touch,
By thinking, "We must not expect too much."

The blind man's neighbors are blinded by their low expectations. They do not believe much, expect much, or get much: "Is this not the man who used to sit and beg?" (v. 9). The change brought about by the touch of the Lord Jesus is so powerful and dramatic that his neighbors find it difficult to believe he is the same person. Concluding it could not possibly be the former beggar, some say, "It is someone like him." The man keeps saying, "I am the man" (v. 9).

Is this your life? Are you holding tight to doubt's old wooden crutch? I am persuaded that most of us get out of our relationship with Jesus just about what we expect. Jesus tells us, "According to your faith let it be done to you" (Matthew 9:29).

Blinded by Preconceived Notions

"They brought to the Pharisees the man who had formerly been blind. Now it was a Sabbath day when Jesus made the mud and opened his eyes" (vv. 13-14). The man's neighbors, out of their unbelief, probably insist on this encounter with their religious experts to hear what the Pharisees would make of his testimony about healing. This would be the formerly blind man's first hearing before the Pharisees. When the Pharisees ask how Jesus had healed him, the blind man explains, "He put mud on my eyes. Then I washed, and now I see" (v. 15). Some of them conclude that Jesus could not be from God if he violated the Sabbath. In fact, it is the Pharisees own stringent interpretation of the Sabbath law that is violated. Their conclusion is *a priori* because they start with their own interpretation of the law and apply it to Jesus' healing of the blind man. Others, more impressed by the reality that in their midst is a formerly blind man who now can see, reason in *a posteriori* fashion. That is, they examine the facts and work back to the healing that Jesus performed on the blind man.

Little do those in the first group realize that the one who healed is the one who at time's beginning set the Sabbath apart as a weekly day of liberation that would strengthen us in our relationship with him.

Are you missing out on the best that God is doing because your preconceived notions about God blind you? Paul writes, "I pray that the God of our Lord Jesus Christ, the Father of glory, may give you a spirit of wisdom and revelation as you come to know him, so that, with the eyes of your heart enlightened" (Ephesians 1:17-18). It is the apostle's prayer that we will see beyond the merely physical things of this life. There are few things that will stunt our Christian growth more than an unwillingness to consider the possibility that God can and will do things that break through the boundaries of our imaginations or expectations. Do you live with a critical spirit toward those whose sense of God is different from yours? If you are, there is a real possibility that you will miss some of the good things that God does in our world every day.

For the second time they called the man who had been blind, and they said to him, "Give glory to God! We know that this man is a sinner." He answered, "I do not know whether he is a sinner. One thing I do know, that though I was blind, now I see." They said to him, "What did he do to you? How did he open your eyes?" He answered them, "I have told you already, and you would not listen. Why do you want to hear it again? Do you also want to become his disciples?" Then they reviled him, saying, "You are his disciple, but we are disciples of Moses. We know that God has spoken to Moses, but as for this man, we do not know where he comes from." The man answered, "Here is an astonishing thing! You do not know where he comes from, and yet he opened my eyes. We know that God does not listen to sinners, but he does listen to one who worships him and obeys his will."
(vv. 24-31)

In this second encounter, the Pharisees, considering themselves again to have the last word of God, try to hound this once-blind man into denying his earlier testimony. The Pharisees have determined that Jesus is assuredly not the Messiah but they are forced to acknowledge that he has performed a miracle. They try to persuade the man that to go along with their ideas would "give glory to God." Their hope now is that the healed man would identify some willful action on Jesus' part that they could use to show that the Lord has broken the law of Moses.

By this time, the man knows that what they really want is to gather information against Jesus. He responds to their questions with humor and common sense that suggests the Pharisees really want to become disciples of Jesus. The Pharisees, however, are not just blind to who Jesus is but to the humorous responses of the target of their questions. No doubt the intelligent religious leaders now realized that this former-blind beggar could see through their veiled attempt to frame Jesus. They would not do that this day because a man who came to faith was not willing to go along with their twisted way of thinking.

One Man No Longer Was Blind!

The blind man could see and nobody could ever change his eyes of the direction of his heart. His spiritual journey from darkness to light is seen from the way he progresses in his description of his Savior. He first speaks of his Lord as "The man called Jesus" (v. 11). Next, he speaks of Jesus as "a prophet" (v. 17). Following this he says Jesus is a "man... from God" (v. 37), and finally, "He said, 'Lord, I believe.' And he worshiped him" (v. 38).

His witness is a beautiful example for us. It is not elaborate, just the truth. A witness simply tells what he has experienced. Through these statements, we learn that faith in Jesus often involves stepping-stones of progress. Perhaps in his pilgrimage you see your own growth in grace and are encouraged. Maybe today you need to determine where you are in your relationship with Jesus and go out and grow.

This much we know: What Jesus did for this man, he still does for every man and every woman. I do not know what your need is, but he knows and that is all you need to know for now. If you will give your need to God, he will meet it. Will you do that now and come closer to Jesus who loved you even to a cross?

Lent 5
John 11:1-45

When Lazarus Leaped and Laughed!

Now a certain man was ill, Lazarus of Bethany, the village of Mary and her sister Martha. Mary was the one who anointed the Lord with perfume and wiped his feet with her hair; her brother Lazarus was ill. So the sisters sent a message to Jesus, "Lord, he whom you love is ill." But when Jesus heard it, he said, "This illness does not lead to death; rather it is for God's glory, so that the Son of God may be glorified through it." Accordingly, though Jesus loved Martha and her sister and Lazarus, after having heard that Lazarus was ill, he stayed two days longer in the place where he was. Then after this he said to the disciples, "Let us go to Judea again." The disciples said to him, "Rabbi, the Jews were just now trying to stone you, and are you going there again?" Jesus answered, "Are there not twelve hours of daylight? Those who walk during the day do not stumble, because they see the light of this world. But those who walk at night stumble, because the light is not in them." After saying this, he told them, "Our friend Lazarus has fallen asleep, but I am going there to awaken him." The disciples said to him, "Lord, if he has fallen asleep, he will be all right." Jesus, however, had been speaking about his death, but they thought that he was referring merely to sleep. Then Jesus told them plainly, "Lazarus is dead. For your sake I am glad I was not there, so that you may believe. But let us go to him." Thomas, who was called the Twin, said to his fellow disciples, "Let us also go, that we may die with him." When Jesus arrived, he found that Lazarus had already been in the tomb four days. Now Bethany was near Jerusalem, some two miles away, and many of the Jews had come to Martha and Mary to console them about their brother. When Martha heard that Jesus was coming, she went and met him, while Mary stayed at home. Martha said to Jesus, "Lord, if you had been here, my brother would not have died. But even now I know that God will give you whatever you

ask of him." Jesus said to her, "Your brother will rise again."
Martha said to him, "I know that he will rise again in the resurrection on the last day." Jesus said to her, "I am the resurrection
and the life. Those who believe in me, even though they die,
will live, and everyone who lives and believes in me will never
die. Do you believe this?" She said to him, "Yes, Lord, I believe
that you are the Messiah, the Son of God, the one coming into
the world." When she had said this, she went back and called
her sister Mary, and told her privately, "The Teacher is here and
is calling for you." And when she heard it, she got up quickly
and went to him. Now Jesus had not yet come to the village,
but was still at the place where Martha had met him. The Jews
who were with her in the house, consoling her, saw Mary get
up quickly and go out. They followed her because they thought
that she was going to the tomb to weep there. When Mary came
where Jesus was and saw him, she knelt at his feet and said to
him, "Lord, if you had been here, my brother would not have
died." When Jesus saw her weeping, and the Jews who came
with her also weeping, he was greatly disturbed in spirit and
deeply moved. He said, "Where have you laid him?" They said
to him, "Lord, come and see." Jesus began to weep. So the Jews
said, "See how he loved him!" But some of them said, "Could
not he who opened the eyes of the blind man have kept this man
from dying?" Then Jesus, again greatly disturbed, came to the
tomb. It was a cave, and a stone was lying against it. Jesus said,
"Take away the stone." Martha, the sister of the dead man, said
to him, "Lord, already there is a stench because he has been
dead four days." Jesus said to her, "Did I not tell you that if you
believed, you would see the glory of God?" So they took away
the stone. And Jesus looked upward and said, "Father, I thank
you for having heard me. I knew that you always hear me, but
I have said this for the sake of the crowd standing here, so that
they may believe that you sent me." When he had said this, he
cried with a loud voice, "Lazarus, come out!" The dead man
came out, his hands and feet bound with strips of cloth, and his
face wrapped in a cloth. Jesus said to them, "Unbind him, and
let him go." Many of the Jews therefore, who had come with
Mary and had seen what Jesus did, believed in him.

This gospel according to John is filled with a series of
vivid verbal masterpieces of the genius, glory, and grace of

Jesus Christ, God's Son. Bible scholars have long believed that each of the four New Testament gospels is targeted at a particular group. Matthew writes his gospel to the Jews. We see that in his frequent references to the Old Testament. Mark writes his gospel with the Romans as his primary target. Hence, Mark is succinct and to the point. His is the first written among the four gospels. Mark spares those rushing Romans the finer details of the Lord's life and ministry on earth while at the same time making clear that Jesus Christ is Lord of all. Luke the physician writes to make the message clearer and more relevant for the well-educated Greeks. Consequently, we see the heady physician cover details about Jesus' life and ministry in the finely crafted Greek of a well-schooled man.

John's gospel is different. John's target gospel audience is far broader than those of the first three gospel writers. Some might say that John writes for the leftover people who for one reason or another are not the targets of the other three writers. There is some element of truth in that idea. The truth, however, is that John has the whole world in his mind as he writes. If the Jews, the Romans, or the Greeks read it, that is all well and good. John, however, writes to reach the whole world. "For God so loved the world," John writes, "that he gave his only Son, so that everyone who believes in him may not perish but may have eternal life. Indeed, God did not send the Son into the world to condemn the world, but in order that the world might be saved through him" (John 3:16-17). If the other storytellers write with laser-target accuracy at one group or another, John's shotgun approach is aimed at all the world. It is John who gives us the great "I am" statements from Jesus and it is to one of these that we turn our attention now. Jesus says, "I am the resurrection and the life. Those who believe in me, even though they die, will live, and everyone who lives and believes in me will never die" (v. 25).

This is a claim from Jesus that takes us to a climax of faith in Jesus Christ. Jesus has made claims about his identity before. Now, however, he makes his claim about his authority over life *and* death, humanity's last great enemy. He makes his claim in the context of the most powerful demonstration of his identity that he had ever made. What is more, we learn from what we are told here that Jesus Christ is deserving of your trust and he can and will make a difference in your life for now and for eternity. We also learn that we do not need to live our lives in a constant state of uncertainty and unhappiness, for we have a victory that money can never buy and that is received in only one way.

Devastation!

"Many of the Jews had come to Martha and Mary to console them about their brother" (v. 19). Lazarus, the brother of Mary and Martha, had died and his death had touched their whole community. Their Jewish background taught them that death was the final and insurmountable defeat for all the living. For the community, and especially for Mary and Martha, life had been crushed by defeat, discouragement, disillusionment, and devastation. As far as they knew, they would never see their beloved brother again. Their Jewish tradition exhorted them to properly mourn the passing of a loved one and prescribed the practices and rituals that would help give expression to their feelings of loss and grief. Somehow the law always seemed to come up short because death was understood to be such a final thing. It would not have mattered what their religion was because there is no religion in the world that can help us face death. Religion is humanity's attempt to reach God but Christianity is not a religion. Christianity is all about God's attempt to reach people. No great world religion offers any easy way to cope with a loved one dying. We do not know but we might imagine that among the emotions of that dark moment when Lazarus died, there could be found guilt for what had been said or done or perhaps left unsaid and undone. Any pastor can tell you that these emotions are often among those experienced when a loved one dies. Death is a reprehensible happening. It tears apart families and friendships. No matter how many ways we try to disguise it and cover it over, death is an awful event and we do as much as we can to pretend it really is not there. There is a school of thought within some Christian circles that almost views death as such a blessing that tears are inappropriate for those who are experiencing the loss of a loved one. However, in the Bible death is an enemy that destroys relationships. It is ugly. It is to be feared and it is repulsive.

What is more, death is universal. None of us will get out of this world alive! The Bible repeatedly makes this point. After Adam sinned in the Garden of Eden, God said to him, "By the sweat of your face you shall eat bread until you return to the ground, for out of it you were taken; you are dust, and to dust you shall return" (Genesis 3:19). Paul by way of affirmation, applies that death sentence to us all: "Just as sin came into the world through one man, and death came through sin, and so death spread to all because all have sinned" (Romans 5:12). The writer to the Hebrews further affirms the universality of death in these words, "It is appointed for mortals to die once, and after that the judgment" (Hebrews 9:27). We used to say that there is nothing certain but death and taxes but we all know about people who have found ways to avoid paying their taxes. So we are left with death as the one great inescapable reality for every person who ever lives. Today each of us is one day closer to dying than we were yesterday and if we survive through the night, tomorrow we will be one day closer to dying than we were when we woke up this morning. Have you calculated that into your plans for your life?

Ben Franklin lived a colorful life and created an amazing

legacy that has touched all our lives. We find his name not only on the Declaration of Independence but on our money, on warships, postage stamps, and perhaps no other person in history has so many towns, counties, educational institutions, and countless other cultural references named for him. There is no record of him ever professing to be a Christian. Nevertheless, in one of his lighter moments he considered his certain death and wrote an imaginary epitaph for himself that seems to have been influenced by the teachings of the apostle Paul. He wrote this:

> The body of B. Franklin, Printer
> Like the Cover of an old Book
> Its contents torn out,
> And stripped of all its Lettering and Gilding,
> Lies here, Food for Worms.
> But the work shall not be wholly lost,
> For it will, as he believed,
> Appear once more
> In a new and more perfect Edition,
> Corrected and amended by the Author.

Although we know that death is universal and certain, many of us seem to make no plans for when it will come to us. One old story tells about a man who attempted to make a deal with Death. He told Death that he would happily go with him when it came time for him to die on one condition. That condition was that Death would send an emissary well in advance to alert him that Death was coming closer. The deal was set. Days became weeks, weeks rolled into months that rolled into years. Finally, one dark night as the man sat alone proudly counting all his achievements and accomplishments, Death suddenly entered the man's room and tapped him on the shoulder and said that the time had come. The man was stunned and argued, "Death, I thought that we had an agreement. You are here with no prior warning. You said you would send an emissary!" Looking that man in the eyes, Death responded, "I have kept my end of our deal. I have sent you many emissaries. Look in your mirror and you will see some of them." The man arose and walked over to his bedroom mirror and as he stood there looking at himself, Death whispered, "Look at your hair that once was black and full and wavy but now it is white and thin and sparse. Notice how you must lean your head toward me to hear my voice because your hearing is not what it once was. See how closely you must stand to the mirror in order to see yourself clearly. Oh, my emissaries have been coming steadily through the years. I'm sorry you did not heed them. Nevertheless, your appointment time is here and we must go."

Please don't get caught out. James reminds us of the brevity of life, "What is your life? For you are a mist that appears for a little while and then vanishes" (James 4:14). The only man Jesus ever called a fool was that rich man who reasoned that he had no place to store all the wealth that he had been able to gather and said,

> I will do this: "I will pull down my barns and build larger ones, and there I will store all my grain and my goods. And I will say to my soul, 'Soul, you have ample goods laid up for many years; relax, eat, drink, be merry.' " Then, said Jesus, "God said to him, 'You fool! This very night your life is being demanded of you. And the things you have prepared, whose will they be?' "
> (Luke 12:18-20)

Sudden illness such as heart attacks, strokes, or accidents in our homes or in our cars, or events we might never imagine can come and take us out of this world instantaneously. The Old Testament Amos counsels us well when he says, "Prepare to meet your God" (Amos 4:12). To fail to heed these words can lead us, as it did Lazarus' family and friends, to our own moment of defeat, discouragement, disillusionment, and devastation.

Dominion!

Jesus said to her, "I am the resurrection and the life. Those who believe in me, even though they die, will live, and everyone who lives and believes in me will never die" (vv. 25-26). In the Bible, death is an enemy that destroys relationships. It is ugly. It is to be feared and it is repulsive. But death does not have the last word. We have a Savior who has the last word over death and says, "I am the resurrection and the life. Those who believe in me, even though they die, will live, and everyone who lives and believes in me will never die" (v. 25). Making such a statement sets Jesus Christ apart from every other person who has existed in the history of the world. In fact, had Jesus never done another miracle than to raise Lazarus, he would stand apart from all the other people who ever walked on earth.

What gives Jesus the right to make such an assertion? Consider what the Bible says about him: He raised other dead people. People like the twelve-year-old daughter of the synagogue leader Jairus. The record says that Jesus "took her by the hand and said to her, 'Talitha cum,' which means, 'Little girl, get up!' And immediately the girl got up and began to walk about" (Mark 5:41-42). There was also the son of the widow of Nain. When Jesus saw the young man's funeral procession, he touched the bier and said, " 'Young man, I say to you, rise!' The dead man sat up and began to speak, and Jesus gave him to his mother" (Luke 7:14-15). Consider also his own resurrection after his abominable death on calvary's cross: The angel said to the women, "Do not be afraid; I know that you are looking for Jesus who was crucified. He is not here; for he has been raised, as he said" (Matthew 28:5-6).

Jesus promises to raise all his followers from the dead and Paul notes this promise in his mighty death conquering chapter:

Since death came through a human being, the resurrection of the dead has also come through a human being; for as all die in Adam, so all will be made alive in Christ. But each in his own order: Christ the first fruits, then at his coming those who belong to Christ.

(1 Corinthians 15:21-23)

All who have taken Christ as their personal Savior can live in the confidence that death is not for us the end of life. We face death with Christ's own assurance that we shall never die.

"Do you believe this?" (John 11:26)

"She said to him, 'Yes, Lord, I believe that you are the Messiah, the Son of God, the one coming into the world' " (v. 27). This question directed at Martha, the sister of Lazarus, is now directed to each of us. As Jesus expected her to affirm her belief, so he expects the same from us. Do we believe him? Do we know beyond a shadow of doubt that if we should die this very day we will spend eternity not in the grave but with Jesus in heaven? When we truly believe this, everything else in life becomes of secondary importance, and we live our lives in confidence and triumphant hope as the people of the certain resurrection.

"The dead man came out, his hands and feet bound with strips of cloth, and his face wrapped in a cloth. Jesus said to them, 'Unbind him, and let him go' " (v. 44).

Eugene O'Neill wrote a creative play that he called *Lazarus Laughed*. It's about Lazarus' life after Jesus raised him from the dead. Guests from Bethany gather for a banquet to honor Lazarus near the beginning of the play. They are all anxious to hear what Lazarus has to say about his experience. As they take their seats, one guest says, "The whole look of his face has changed. He is like a stranger from a far land. There is no longer any sorrow in his eyes. He must have forgotten sorrow in the grave." Another guest, one who had helped roll the tombstone aside, recalls the scene after Jesus raised Lazarus from the dead in even more beautiful terms: "And then Lazarus knelt and kissed Jesus' feet, and both of them smiled, and Jesus blessed him and called him 'My Brother' and went away. And Lazarus, looking after him, began to laugh softly like a man in love with God. Such a laugh I never heard! It made my ears drunk! It was like wine! And though I was half-dead with fright, I found myself laughing too."

Now, I will grant you that the Bible does not record the moment when Lazarus had his grave wrappings removed but I believe that Eugene O'Neill probably got it right. How could anyone being raised from the dead by the Lord of all life ever be sad again? I can imagine not only that Lazarus laughed but that he leaped with great joy for his whole life had not only been restored, it had been enriched in ways beyond words. Can't you imagine that Lazarus lived out the rest of his days with a song of praise in his heart? Can't you imagine that we would do the same?

My closing question for you has two parts. First, the Jesus question: "Do you believe this?" Second, this: Why don't we each go out from now on as people of the resurrection with a song of praise for Jesus in our hearts?

Passion / Palm Sunday
Matthew 26:14—27:66

Live Spelled Backward!

Then one of the twelve, who was called Judas Iscariot, went to the chief priests and said, "What will you give me if I betray him to you?" They paid him thirty pieces of silver. And from that moment he began to look for an opportunity to betray him. On the first day of Unleavened Bread the disciples came to Jesus, saying, "Where do you want us to make the preparations for you to eat the Passover?" He said, "Go into the city to a certain man, and say to him, 'The Teacher says, My time is near; I will keep the Passover at your house with my disciples.' " So the disciples did as Jesus had directed them, and they prepared the Passover meal. When it was evening, he took his place with the twelve; and while they were eating, he said, "Truly I tell you, one of you will betray me." And they became greatly distressed and began to say to him one after another, "Surely not I, Lord?" He answered, "The one who has dipped his hand into the bowl with me will betray me. The Son of Man goes as it is written of him, but woe to that one by whom the Son of Man is betrayed! It would have been better for that one not to have been born." Judas, who betrayed him, said, "Surely not I, Rabbi?" He replied, "You have said so." While they were eating, Jesus took a loaf of bread, and after blessing it he broke it, gave it to the disciples, and said, "Take, eat; this is my body." Then he took a cup, and after giving thanks he gave it to them, saying, "Drink from it, all of you..."

In a CBS News *60 Minutes* interview, U.S. Supreme Court Justice Sonia Sotomayor was asked why she had resigned as an Assistant District Attorney for the Bronx. She replied, "Because for the first time in my life I saw evil first hand and I felt that if I stayed that close to it, it just might rub off on me."[1] Come think with me about an age-old human affliction that has impacted the life of every person ever born and the two people who were not born but created in the Garden of Eden, a thing called evil. Justice Sonia Sotomayor feared that it might rub off on her.

Let me ask you a question: Have you ever encountered evil? Do you know anything about the machinations of evil? In his book *People of the Lie*,[2] the late American psychiatrist Scott Peck discusses evil. According to Dr. Peck, evil people are consistently self-deceiving with the intent of avoiding guilt and maintaining a self-image of perfection and are characterized not so much by the magnitude of their sins, but by their consistently destructive practices. This syndrome results in a projection of evil onto selected innocent people who are seen only as play things or tools to be manipulated. This is the paradoxical mechanism by which evil people, Peck's "people of the lie," commit their despicable deeds. Sonia Sotomayor says as an Assistant District Attorney she saw evil. Psychiatrist Peck writes that such people are rarely seen by psychiatrists. He further asserts that psychiatry has no successful treatment plans for evil people. I submit that only the gospel of Jesus Christ can overcome evil as we see, in fact, that happened repeatedly while Jesus walked among us.

E-V-I-L! Scott Peck used to tell the story of how he, a highly regarded scholar and writer, was struggling to find a succinct definition of evil for his *People of the Lie* book. His then eight-year-old son, noticing the expression on his father's face, asked his daddy what was troubling him. "I'm trying to define evil." "That's easy," the son replied, "evil is LIVE spelled backward!" That is what it is!

So I would speak today about LIFE lived in reverse gear, perverted goodness that does the right things for the wrong reasons. Evil is demonstrated in misplaced self-focused passion, negative, critical spirituality, love running in the wrong direction, a phenomenon that hurts our humanity and defaces our divinity. Have you ever experienced evil? Have you seen it in your own life? Or in the life of someone else? Do you know anything about personal iniquity? Have you ever been victimized by systemic sin? Evil is live spelled backward.

Evil's Genesis

From what perverted place did evil emanate? According to the book of God's revelation, it showed up initially in a certain garden. The Genesis record says in substance that evil presented itself in serpentine form to Eve, the grandmother of all living. There, in that garden, what was a rapturous relationship between the Creator and the creature was ruptured and riveted into a raucous reality. But is that garden really the only locus of evil's genesis? I'm afraid not.

If we really want to look at evil's nefarious beginnings we must look up. Up past where the eagles play; up beyond the sun, the moon, and the stars; all the way up to a throne room in glory where cherubim chant and seraphim sing; where elders cry out, "Holy! Holy! Holy! Lord God of hosts." Isaiah tells us that evil began there.

Lucifer, one of heaven's angels, desired to usurp the established divine authority and had the temerity to say, "I will ascend to heaven; I will raise my throne above the stars of God... I will ascend to the tops of the clouds, I will make myself like the Most High" (Isaiah 14:13-14). After that, God was forced to expel Lucifer from the heavenly habitat and Lucifer, whose name means "light," fell into dark ways. He plummeted downward from the home of grace. Yet, when he fell, he did not fall all the way. He came down but he did not crash. His fall was halted somewhere between high enough from earth and low enough from heaven for him to receive the title "Prince of the power of the air" (Ephesians 2:2 ESV). He descended from heaven and fell just high enough to set up shop where he could deputize emissaries for the purpose of reaping havoc among us, our forbears, and generations not yet born. That, according to the Bible, is where evil found its origins and where its roots are found today. So we can say that it is no surprise that psychiatry has not yet found a cure for it.

Evil Personified

The most pronounced human example of this diabolical thing called evil is a certain man named Judas Iscariot. An old preacher said, "Don't ever preach about Judas for to do that only gives him free advertising." We must look at Judas because he so incarnates the evil that we consider just now. Moreover, we must look briefly in the direction of the evil Judas to catch a deeper understanding of how far unrequited evil can carry a person.

Have you ever wondered why Jesus Christ, Son of the living God, would choose a man like Judas to be a disciple in the first place? Has that question not crept up at least to the outskirts of your mind? Why would he choose a man in whom he surely knew there was a devil? Jesus knew what he was doing. I read of him asking, "Have I not chosen twelve and one of you is a devil?" (John 6:70). Why would heaven's darling and earth's Savior bring into the ranks of the disciples and give momentary credibility to such a grand rascal as Judas Iscariot? Why? I believe Jesus brought Judas into the ranks of the disciples for several reasons that I would like to share with you.

Choosing Evil

First, Jesus allowed Judas to be part of the twelve to demonstrate evil's omnipresence. Jesus wants us to understand that clearly. Now to speak about evil's omnipresence is not to include heaven in that definition of omnipresence for the moment. What we mean is that there is no place south of heaven where evil is not to be found. You may remember, for example, the experience recorded in Job's life where the sons of God come to present themselves before God himself. Do you remember also who comes with them? It is the bold Satan. Scripture says, God interrogated him: "Satan, where have you come from?" "Well, God, I've just been going to and fro throughout the earth." "For what purpose, Satan?" "Well, seeking whom I may devour" (cf. Job 1:7ff). Then a little later the sons of God come again to present themselves. God looks and Satan is still there. Again God asks, "Satan, where are you coming from?" "Same place, going to and fro throughout the earth seeking whom I may devour. God, you really don't have to worry about me. I'm not like these mortals created in your image. I am, if nothing else, consistent."

Evil is everywhere all the time. He was "among the sons of God." He is even within the confines of the church of the living God. But, you knew that, didn't you? Sometimes we Christians make the mistake of thinking Satan is working hardest in places he long ago left. He does not need to hang out in the so-called "worldly" places. His weeds of evil are well planted there and now are producing their godless harvest. They are "back-to-nature" gardens that no longer need tending. He has already taken possession of them and left them on a kind of Holy Spirit-less autopilot. His primary place of action today is within the church. In his *The Screwtape Letters*,[3] C.S. Lewis has the devil Screwtape instruct his nephew, Wormwood, the apprentice demon, that if he really wants to disrupt God's work on earth the best place to do that is from inside the church. So Wormwood is told to become involved in the inner workings of the church with the express intent of ingratiating himself so that he might begin his destructive work from the inside. Satan comes wherever God's people gather. He comes on time. He comes before time. He likes a good seat. He gets himself on church boards and committees. He becomes an usher so he can greet well-intentioned worshipers with his sour and surly spirit.

He sings in the choir. Martin Luther once said, "When the devil fell, he fell into the choir loft." Luther understood the power of music. He wrote hymns in order to teach the gospel with song. The choir sings in order to point us to Jesus. Lucifer was in the heavenly choir when he was expelled. He will even climb up the steps into the pulpit and stand up in sacred space if we are not careful. The question we must ask even of ourselves is, "What motivates us to become involved in the things we do?" There is an interesting line in John's apocalypse about "the synagogue of Satan" (Revelation 3:9 ESV). It makes us wonder if there are some churches where Satan has particular control.

Remember, evil is everywhere. I think the master wanted us to understand the truth of that assertion. What better way to demonstrate that truth than to pick someone like Judas. But there is a second reason why Jesus picked Judas Iscariot to be one of the twelve. He wanted to demonstrate to us that even when given a chance, not everyone would follow good leadership. Jesus chose this son of perdition to show us that even the best leaders will not be universally accepted. After he led the British people to victory from almost certain defeat in World War II, Winston Churchill was rejected by the very people whose lives and livelihood he saved. It should not surprise us when somebody the church has helped breaks ranks. Not everyone will fall in line and march straight. Jesus selected Judas Iscariot to demonstrate that not everyone will follow sound leadership. Judas was with the Son of God for three years. It was three years of exposure to perfect goodness and unfeigned love; three years with the light of the world; three years with the finest example of humanity who ever set foot on this planet. Three years and every day of it counted for naught with Judas! Perhaps Jesus chose Judas to show us that mere physical proximity is no proof of spiritual similarity. One can be close to the fire and be as spiritually cold as a winter day in the Arctic Circle. Sometimes those who have been in the church for a long time do not have the foggiest notion of what the church, God's kingdom, is about. Close proximity is no sign of spiritual nearness, and Jesus wants us to understand that not everyone will necessarily follow good leadership.

There is more. I believe that the Lord of life selected Judas Iscariot in whom he knew there was a devil for a third reason: namely, to encourage his church with the truth that good is more potent than evil. Most of us tend to agree with Mark Anthony who declared that "the good that men do is often interred with their bones while the evil that men do lives after them." That, however, is not necessarily so. Paul instructs us, "Do not be overcome by evil, but overcome evil with good" (Romans 12:21). In the kingdom good is far stronger than evil. Do you realize that in three years Judas did not succeed in winning a single convert to his way of thinking? Not one! Knowing how the devil operates, we can be sure that it was not for want of trying.

Imagine, if you will, Judas on some evenings when the Mediterranean humidity was thick and Jesus and his men exhausted from the intensity of a long day, tried to snatch some sleep. Here comes Judas, the human embodiment of Satan who never sleeps, easing up, saying to Thomas, and shaking him out of his sleep. "Wake up, Thomas," he whispers, "I want to talk with you. I have observed you, Thomas. You have a sharp mind. You are a thinker, Thomas. Thomas, don't you think Jesus has got this thing all wrong? I remember, Thomas, that day out in the hills of Tiberius when Jesus spoke about feeding that multitude. You thought that was an ill-conceived idea. Yes, you are real smart, Thomas, not driven by emotions like Peter but a thinker." I'm sure he tried to convince Thomas, a man given to doubts and fears. "Thomas, don't you think he is a little crazy, going around here stirring up people?" And Thomas said, "I've thought that on occasion, but every time I decide that it's a foolish pursuit following him, he does something new that astounds me and I want to follow him anew."

Don't you know he must have tried to win over Peter, next to Jesus the leader of the group: "Peter, you are the man! Don't you think he is headed for failure? It is just a matter of time, Peter. Now he's talking about taking on Caiaphas and that temple crowd in Jerusalem. He is about to get us sandwiched between the religion of Jerusalem and the politics of Rome. Peter, don't you think Jesus is crazy?" Can you hear Peter saying to Judas, the devil wearing human skin, "I've been on the verge of that thought from time to time. Then when I start thinking like that he does something to demonstrate he is more than a conqueror." Yes, Jesus chose Judas to demonstrate that good is ultimately more potent than evil.

I can imagine that Jesus selected Judas for at least one other reason. He wanted to teach us how to deal with evil. Come with me to Bethany, on the Mount of Olives. It is the last Thursday Jesus will be the Son of Man. Already the shades of evening are beginning to fall and he stands there in the company of his disciples and looks across Kidron Valley to the city of his destiny, Jerusalem. He looks the twelve in the eye and says, "It's marching time." They move out from Bethany, down through the valley, past the olive groves to the city of David, where they enter the gate and amble through cobblestone streets until they come at last to what someone once called "a narrow house on a dead-end street."

They enter that house and go up the stairs to the second story. Once there, they go into an upper room. Remember, it was an Upper Room. Plant that line firmly in your thinking. It was an Upper Room. One of my favorite preachers, the late Dr. William A. Jones, told me a story out of his native Kentucky. He said that up in the mountains there is an interesting thing called the "snake line." Experienced hunters know the elevation of the snake line, not because they have gone around the mountains and drawn a white line and put a "snake line" label on it. Experienced hunters, according to Dr. Jones, just know the elevation of the snake line. When hunters go on a hunt, they always pitch their tents above that snake line so that while the hunter sleeps rattlesnakes and other poisonous creatures will not come around to inflict harm and possibly death. Snakes cannot survive above the snake line.

It was the Upper Room. Jesus led the disciples up above the snake line. There sitting around the table they celebrated the Passover meal and Jesus announced, "One of you will betray me." Judas, the snake, could not last in that environment. He stayed for the feast then left in a hurry. Judas left. He fled to some other snakes and strategized as to how he would inflict his poison.

Evil's End

Judas "hanged himself!" (Matthew 27:5). Given time, evil always hangs itself. Christian, listen: You will never have to get even with anybody. You do not have to retaliate. You do not need to waste your time and energy worrying about people possessed of serpentine spirits.

Take them Up! Up! Up! Up in prayer. Up in love. Up above the snake line. Do not live your life in reverse. Do not take up residence where the snakes abide. Always live your life going forward and along the way sing to yourself,

> I'm pressing on the upward way;
> New heights I'm gaining every day;
> Still praying as I onward bound,
> Lord, plant my feet on higher ground.
>
> Lord, lift me up and let me stand;
> By faith on heaven's table land,
> A higher plane than I have found;
> Lord, plant my feet on higher ground.

My heart has no desire to stay;
Where doubts arise and fears dismay;
Though some may dwell where these abound;
My prayer, My aim, is higher ground.
— Johnson Oatman Jr., 1898 (public domain)

---

1. CBS News *60 Minutes* broadcast on January 13, 2013.

2. Dr. Scott Peck, *People of the Lie: The Hope for Healing Human Evil* (New York: Simon & Schuster, 1983).

3. C.S. Lewis, *The Screwtape Letters* (New York: HarperCollins, 2001).

Maundy Thursday
John 13:1-17, 31b-35

No Greater Love!

Now before the festival of the Passover, Jesus knew that his hour had come to depart from this world and go to the Father. Having loved his own who were in the world, he loved them to the end. The devil had already put it into the heart of Judas son of Simon Iscariot to betray him. And during supper Jesus, knowing that the Father had given all things into his hands, and that he had come from God and was going to God, got up from the table, took off his outer robe, and tied a towel around himself. Then he poured water into a basin and began to wash the disciples' feet and to wipe them with the towel that was tied around him. He came to Simon Peter, who said to him, "Lord, are you going to wash my feet?" Jesus answered, "You do not know now what I am doing, but later you will understand." Peter said to him, "You will never wash my feet." Jesus answered, "Unless I wash you, you have no share with me." Simon Peter said to him, "Lord, not my feet only but also my hands and my head!" Jesus said to him, "One who has bathed does not need to wash, except for the feet, but is entirely clean. And you are clean, though not all of you." For he knew who was to betray him; for this reason he said, "Not all of you are clean." After he had washed their feet, had put on his robe, and had returned to the table, he said to them, "Do you know what I have done to you? You call me Teacher and Lord — and you are right, for that is what I am. So if I, your Lord and Teacher, have washed your feet, you also ought to wash one another's feet. For I have set you an example, that you also should do as I have done to you. Very truly, I tell you, servants are not greater than their master, nor are messengers greater than the one who sent them. If you know these things, you are blessed if you do them..." Jesus said, "Now the Son of Man has been glorified, and God has been glorified in him. If God has been glorified in him, God will also glorify him in himself and will glorify him at once. Little children, I am with you only a little longer. You will look for me; and as I said to the Jews so now I say to you, 'Where I am going, you cannot come.' I give you a new commandment, that you love one another. Just as I have loved you, you also should love one another. By this everyone will know that you are my disciples, if you have love for one another."

"When Jesus Christ calls a man, he bids him, 'Come and die!' " Dietrich Bonhoeffer, the German pastor and theologian wrote that sentence in his cell on April 9, 1945. He was within hours of the hangman's rope being placed around his neck in the Flossenbürg concentration camp in Nazi Germany. Son of a leading authority on psychology, neurology, and a university professor, as a young man Dietrich had turned away from the life of prestige and privilege that would naturally befall him in order to pursue his sense of call to become a pastor. When the Third Reich came into power, Bonhoeffer could have chosen to stay in the United States and teach at the seminary where he had just earned his doctorate. Instead, he was moved with love for the Christians of his homeland and returned there to become the pastor of a small Lutheran congregation. He ended up dying on the end of a hangman's rope primarily because of his love for God, for God's people, and the land of his birth. Jesus says, "I give you a new commandment, that you love one another. Just as I have loved you, you also should love one another. By this everyone will know that you are my disciples, if you have love for one another" (vv. 34-35).

What sets the church of Jesus Christ apart from any other organization in the world? The answer is two things: First, the Christian church is the only society in the world that requires its members to admit that they are sinners and do not deserve to be members. Second, the church of Jesus is the only organization that demands of its members they possess this amazing love that we will call a "love in spite of." Just before his crucifixion, Jesus identified the primary evidence that would set his disciples apart from the rest of the world. He issued what he termed "a new commandment." This command to "love one another" would at the same time reflect Christ's own love for us and signify to the world that we are his disciples.

Knowing this, of course, immediately raises a series of questions. Question number one is do we truly know what kind of love this love is? Question number two is how do we develop this kind of love? Question three is how do we demonstrate this kind of love?

The Definition of this Love

Love to both God and man is fundamental to true Christianity, and we find that idea expressed in the Old Testament and the New Testament. Jesus himself declared that all the law and the prophets hang upon love. The Old Testament taught us that "you shall love your neighbor as yourself" (Leviticus 19:18). Yet Jesus says here that this is "a new commandment." What is different about this love that allows him to call it "new"? Simply this, "Just as I have loved you, you also should love one another" (v. 34). Jesus is calling us to a higher standard of love than the world had ever seen before, a love following the example of his own love for us.

Just what did Jesus' love look like? Jesus explained what he had in mind in these words: "No one has greater love than this, to lay down one's life for one's friends" (John 15:13). Paul, once a warrior against Jesus and now a beloved prisoner of Christ's love, directs the Ephesians and through them, us to "be imitators of God, as beloved children, and live in love, as Christ loved us and gave himself up for us, a fragrant offering and sacrifice to God" (Ephesians 5:1-2). In his epistles, John speaks of it in these words, "We know love by this, that he laid down his life for us — and we ought to lay down our lives for one another. How does God's love abide in anyone who has the world's goods and sees a brother or sister in need and yet refuses help? Little children, let us love, not in word or speech, but in truth and action" (1 John 3:16-18). The early Jerusalem church put it into practice: "All who believed were together and had all things in common; they would sell their possessions and goods and distribute the proceeds to all, as any had need" (Acts 2:44-45).

You and I are called to make this love observable to the whole world: "By this everyone will know that you are my disciples, if you have love for one another" (John 13:35). To fulfill this command and allow the world to see this love we must allow this love to be seen outside the church building and in the everyday interactions of the Lord's people.

The Development of this Love

If we are to show off this amazing love that Jesus modeled for us, how will it begin to grow in and through us? Paul says that we are taught to love like this by God himself:

> Now concerning love of the brothers and sisters, you do not need to have anyone write to you, for you yourselves have been taught by God to love one another; and indeed you do love all the brothers and sisters throughout Macedonia. But we urge you, beloved, to do so more and more.
> (1 Thessalonians 4:9-10)

We have a sense of the depth of God's love earlier in John's gospel when we read, "God so loved the world that he gave his only Son" (John 3:16). Now, reflect on that phrase for a moment... for what would you be willing to sacrifice a child? God sacrificed his Son out of love for us and "while we still were sinners Christ died for us" (Romans 5:8). John affirms this in his first epistle, "This is love, not that we loved God but that he loved us and sent his Son to be the atoning sacrifice for our sins" (1 John 4:10). So this love begins its development in us when we think about the love of God the Father.

This love develops further when we begin to model the love of God the Son, Jesus. Once again we find the instruction from John's first epistle — not now from John 3:16 but from 1 John 3:16: "We know love by this, that he laid down his life for us — and we ought to lay down our lives for one another." Surely the closer we walk to Jesus, the more we will want to follow, to the best of our ability, the model of his life and ministry and love as he loved.

Then this love develops further again as we model it, and see it modeled, among the people of the church. "Let us consider how to provoke one another to love and good deeds" (Hebrews 10:24). This statement from the writer to the Hebrews moves love from the vertical to the horizontal dimension of everyday Christian living. There is a distinct parallel between the time when this epistle was written and what is happening in our day. Back then, some people were relinquishing their faith and their connection with God's people in the church, so the Hebrews were instructed to "provoke" or stimulate love between one another. And just like today, regular attendance at church meetings facilitates love for one another because there we receive reminders and exhortations to persevere in our love just as Jesus perseveres in his love for us. As we do this, love develops.

The Demonstration of this Love

While a college student, Heidi Neumark, now a Lutheran pastor, took a year off from her studies at Brown University to be part of a volunteer program sponsored by a group called Rural Mission. She was sent to Johns Island — off the Carolina coast — where she learned from the sons and daughters of plantation slaves who allowed her to listen in as they sat around telling stories.

In Heidi's own words:

The most important lesson I learned on Johns Island was from Miss Ellie, who lived miles down a small dirt road in a one-room, wooden home. I loved to visit her. We'd sit in old rocking chairs on the front porch, drinking tall glasses of sweet tea, while she'd tell me stories punctuated with Gullah expressions that would leap from her river of thought like bright, silver fish: "Girl, I be so happy I could jump the sky!" I never could find out Miss Ellie's precise age, but it was somewhere between 90 and 100. Maybe she didn't know herself. She still chopped her own firewood, stacked in neat little piles behind the house. Miss Ellie had a friend named Netta whom she'd known since they were small girls. In order to get to Netta's house, Miss Ellie had to walk for miles through fields of tall grass. This was the sweet grass that Sea Island women make famous baskets out of, but it was also home to numerous poisonous snakes: coral snakes, rattlesnakes, water moccasins, and copperheads. Actually, Netta's home was not that far from Miss Ellie's place, but there was a stream that cut across the fields. You had to walk quite a distance to get to the place where it narrowed enough to pass. I admired Miss Ellie, who would set off to visit her friend full of bouncy enthusiasm, with no worry for the snakes or the long miles. I also felt sorry for her. Poor Miss Ellie, I thought, old and arthritic, having to walk all that way, pushing through the thick summer heat, not to mention the snakes. I felt sorry — until I hit upon the perfect plan. I arranged with some men to help build a simple plank bridge across the stream near Miss Ellie's house. I scouted out the ideal place — not too wide, but too deep to cross. I bought and helped carry the planks there myself. Our bridge was built in a day. I was so excited that I could hardly wait to see Miss Ellie's reaction. I went to her house, where she wanted to sit in her rocker and tell stories, but I was too impatient with my project. I practically dragged her off with me. "Look!" I shouted, "a shortcut for you to visit Netta!" Miss Ellie's face did not register the grateful, happy look I expected. There was no smile, no jumping the sky. Instead, for a long time, she looked puzzled, then she shook her head and looked at me as though I were the one who needed pity. "Child, I don't need a shortcut." And she told about all the friends she kept up with on her way to visit Netta. A shortcut would cut her off from Mr. Jenkins, with whom she always swapped gossip; from Miss

Hunter, who so looked forward to the quilt scraps she'd bring by; from the raisin wine she'd taste at one place in exchange for her biscuits; and the chance to look in on the "old folks" who were sick. "Child," she said again, "can't take shortcuts if you want friends in this world. Shortcuts don't mix with love."[1]

She was right, love sometimes calls for us to be prepared to take the longer route. Jesus says, "By this everyone will know that you are my disciples, if you have love for one another." When the church meets, and especially when we see visitors present, we have an opportunity to demonstrate the love of Jesus before them. It is important that people who stop in to observe the church in action see genuine Christ-like love exercised among church people. So we can ask ourselves whether we are truly happy to see our brothers and sisters in worship and does our demonstrated consistent sincerity of our love help others who are not yet disciples to see that the love we find in Jesus is no ordinary love?

Another place where the people of the church have an opportunity to show true Jesus love is when we are outside the four walls of the church in our community. A Christian family traveling on a European vacation boarded a train from London to Dover in England. In Dover, they were scheduled to board a hovercraft that would ferry them across the English Channel to Calais, France. From there they were scheduled to board another train to Paris. It was a trip of a lifetime that they had planned for a long time. After the train pulled into the station at Dover, the passengers began to disembark. Suddenly, one man's overloaded suitcase burst open on the train station platform and almost all the contents fell onto the ground. The wind blew some of the contents across the platform. Even though the connection between train and hovercraft allowed only a few minutes, that family stopped on the platform and helped the man gather up his belongings and repack them. As they packed, the distraught man kept telling them that they might be too late to connect with the hovercraft, but they assured him that they were willing to risk that to help him. After all the contents of the case were gathered and the suitcase was repacked, the family and their new friend, his suitcase held together with a leather belt from his pants, rushed toward the dock. They arrived just in time to board. As they walked down the pier to the hovercraft the man said, "I've got it. You must be Christians." "Why would you say that?" the dad asked. "Because," said the man whose suitcase had burst, "you put my needs before your own priorities." As it turned out, the man was a former highly involved Christian worker who, as the result of certain life circumstances, had been shunned by his former fellowship after a divorce that he tried to prevent and had left his faith. That day, he was one of the "everyone" Jesus spoke about and he witnessed firsthand how the love of Jesus works itself out when a suitcase bursts on a railway platform even when the schedule is tight. Before their visit ended, the man used his influence to help that family enjoy special access to Notre Dame and the Eiffel Tower. More important, he promised the helpful family that he would start attending church again.

What does "everyone," those people outside the church, see in each of us? Do they see people who are forgiving? Do they find people who hold on to old wounds and grudges? Do they see a sincere interest in the well-being of other people? Or do they see indifference to the needs of others? Do they see the church divided against itself, or its people standing together in unity and love?

Methodist bishop William Willimon in his book, *The Theology and Practice of Ordained Ministry*, writes, "Not long before his death, Martin Luther King Jr. spoke to the congregation at Atlanta's Ebenezer Baptist Church: 'If any of you are around when I have to meet my day, I don't want a long funeral. And if you get somebody to deliver the eulogy, tell them not to talk too long. Every now and then

I wonder what I want them to say. Tell them not to mention that I have a Nobel Peace Prize; that isn't important. Tell them not to mention that I have three or four hundred other awards; that's not important. Tell them not to mention where I went to school. I'd like somebody to mention that day that Martin Luther King Jr. tried to love somebody.' "[2]

In the wonderful classic movie *Spartacus*, which retells the historical account of the great Roman slave rebellion in 71 BC, Spartacus (played by Kirk Douglas) was a highly trained gladiator who escaped and led other slaves to freedom. As news of his rebellion grew, thousands of slaves joined his cause and followed him through victories and defeats. Near the end of the movie, a massive Roman army, under the command of Senator Crassus (masterfully played by Laurence Olivier), captures the rebels. Although Crassus does not know what Spartacus looks like, he suspects that Spartacus is alive among the prisoners under guard. In full Roman uniform, Crassus gallops up to the mouth of the valley where the prisoners are being held and shouts an offer to them: they can escape death by crucifixion if they turn Spartacus over to him. Spartacus studies the ground for several seconds and then boldly rises to his feet, planning to turn himself in. But before he can open his mouth to say who he is, his friend to his left stands and calls out, "I am Spartacus!" Then another on his right also stands and calls out, "I am Spartacus!" As the real Spartacus looks on, comrade after comrade in his slave army rises to their feet and calls out, "I am Spartacus!" until there is a chorus of thousands united. These slaves show what it means to be the church — standing as one and identifying with our Lord even though it could mean our own end.

Jesus who loved us all the way to calvary's cross did not say to us, "Here is the mark of being my disciple, gather around you a crowd of thousands of people and preach until you see hundreds of them profess their salvation." Instead he said, "If I, your Lord and Teacher, have washed your feet, you also ought to wash one another's feet" (v. 14). Then he said, "I give you a new commandment, that you love one another. Just as I have loved you, you also should love one another. By this everyone will know that you are my disciples, if you have love for one another" (vv. 34-35). Ask yourself how you will show this love each time you have an opportunity.

---

1. *Breathing Space*, adapted from Heidi Neumark (Boston: Beacon Press, 2003), pp. 16-17.

2. William Willimon, *Pastor: The Theology and Practice of Ordained Ministry* (Nashville: Abingdon Press, 2002), p. 53.

Good Friday
John 18:1—19:42

Son of a Daddy!

After Jesus had spoken these words, he went out with his disciples across the Kidron Valley to a place where there was a garden, which he and his disciples entered. Now Judas, who betrayed him, also knew the place, because Jesus often met there with his disciples. So Judas brought a detachment of soldiers together with police from the chief priests and the Pharisees, and they came there with lanterns and torches and weapons. Then Jesus, knowing all that was to happen to him, came forward and asked them, "Whom are you looking for?" They answered, "Jesus of Nazareth." Jesus replied, "I am he." Judas, who betrayed him, was standing with them. When Jesus said to them, "I am he," they stepped back and fell to the ground. Again he asked them, "Whom are you looking for?" And they said, "Jesus of Nazareth." Jesus answered, "I told you that I am he. So if you are looking for me, let these men go." This was to fulfill the word that he had spoken, "I did not lose a single one of those whom you gave me." Then Simon Peter, who had a sword, drew it, struck the high priest's slave, and cut off his right ear. The slave's name was Malchus. Jesus said to Peter, "Put your sword back into its sheath. Am I not to drink the cup that the Father has given me?" So the soldiers, their officer, and the Jewish police arrested Jesus and bound him. First they took him to Annas, who was the father-in-law of Caiaphas, the high priest that year. Caiaphas was the one who had advised the Jews that it was better to have one person die for the people. Simon Peter and another disciple followed Jesus. Since that disciple was known to the high priest, he went with Jesus into the courtyard of the high priest, but Peter was standing outside at the gate. So the other disciple, who was known to the high priest, went out, spoke to the woman who guarded the gate, and brought Peter in. The woman said to Peter, "You are not also one of this man's disciples, are you?" He said, "I am not." Now the slaves and the police had made a charcoal fire because it was cold, and they were standing around it and warming themselves. Peter also was standing with them and warming himself. Then the high priest questioned Jesus about his disciples and about his teaching. Jesus answered, "I have spoken openly to the world; I have always taught in synagogues and in the temple, where all the Jews come together. I have said nothing in secret. Why do you ask me? Ask those who heard what I said to them; they know what I said." When he had said this, one of the police standing nearby struck Jesus on the face, saying, "Is that how you answer the high priest?" Jesus answered, "If I have spoken wrongly, testify to the wrong. But if I have spoken rightly, why do you strike me?" Then Annas sent him bound to Caiaphas the high priest. Now Simon Peter was standing and warming himself. They asked him, "You are not also one of his disciples, are you?" He denied it and said, "I am not." One of the slaves of the high priest, a relative of the man whose ear Peter had cut off, asked, "Did I not see you in the garden with him?" Again Peter denied it, and at that moment the cock crowed. Then they took Jesus from Caiaphas to Pilate's headquarters. It was early in the morning. They themselves did not enter the headquarters, so as to avoid ritual defilement and to be able to eat the Passover. So Pilate went out to them and said, "What accusation do you bring against this man?" They answered, "If this man were not a criminal, we would not have handed him over to you." Pilate said to them, "Take him yourselves and judge him according to your law." The Jews replied, "We are not permitted to put any-one to death." (This was to fulfill what Jesus had said when he indicated the kind of death he was to die.) Then Pilate entered the headquarters again, summoned Jesus, and asked him, "Are you the King of the Jews?" Jesus answered, "Do you ask this on your own, or did others tell you about me?" Pilate replied, "I am not a Jew, am I? Your own nation and the chief priests have handed you over to me. What have you done?" Jesus answered, "My kingdom is not from this world. If my kingdom were from this world, my followers would be fighting to keep me from being handed over to the Jews. But as it is, my kingdom is not from here." Pilate asked him, "So you are a king?" Jesus an-swered, "You say that I am a king. For this I was born, and for this I came into the world, to testify to the truth. Everyone who belongs to the truth listens to my voice." Pilate asked him, "What is truth?" After he had said this, he went out to the Jews again and told them, "I find no case against him. But you have a custom that I release someone for you at the Passover. Do you want me to release for you the King of the Jews?" They shouted in reply, "Not this man, but Barabbas!" Now Barabbas was a bandit.

Then Pilate took Jesus and had him flogged. And the soldiers wove a crown of thorns and put it on his head, and they dressed him in a purple robe. They kept coming up to him, saying, "Hail, King of the Jews!" and striking him on the face. Pilate went out again and said to them, "Look, I am bringing him out to you to let you know that I find no case against him." So Jesus came out, wearing the crown of thorns and the purple robe. Pilate said to them, "Here is the man!" When the chief priests and the police saw him, they shouted, "Crucify him! Crucify him!" Pilate said to them, "Take him yourselves and crucify him; I find no case against him." The Jews answered him, "We have a law, and according to that law he ought to die because he has claimed to be the Son of God." Now when Pilate heard this, he was more afraid than ever. He entered his headquarters again and asked Jesus, "Where are you from?" But Jesus gave him no answer. Pilate therefore said to him, "Do you refuse to speak to me? Do you not know that I have power to release you, and power to crucify you?" Jesus answered him, "You would have no power over me unless it had been given you from above; therefore the one who handed me over to you is guilty of a greater sin." From then on Pilate tried to release him, but the Jews cried out, "If you release this man, you are no friend of the emperor. Everyone who claims to be a king sets himself against the emperor." When Pilate heard these words, he brought Jesus outside and sat on the judge's bench at a place called The Stone Pavement, or in Hebrew Gabbatha. Now it was the day of Preparation for the Passover; and it was about noon. He said to the Jews, "Here is your King!" They cried out, "Away with him! Away with him! Crucify him!" Pilate asked them, "Shall I crucify your King?" The chief priests answered, "We have no king but the emperor." Then he handed him over to them to be crucified. So they took Jesus; and carrying the cross by himself, he went out to what is called The Place of the Skull, which in Hebrew is called Golgotha. There they crucified him, and with him two others, one on either side, with Jesus between them. Pilate also had an inscription written and put on the cross. It read, "Jesus of Nazareth, the King of the Jews." Many of the Jews read this inscription, because the place where Jesus was crucified was near the city; and it was written in Hebrew, in Latin, and in Greek. Then the chief priests of the Jews said to Pilate, "Do not write, 'The King of the Jews,' but, 'This man said, I am King of the Jews.' " Pilate answered, "What I have written I have written." When the soldiers had crucified Jesus, they took his clothes and divided them into four parts, one for each soldier. They also took his tunic; now the tunic was seamless, woven in one piece from the top. So they said to one another, "Let us not tear it, but cast lots for it to see who will get it." This was to fulfill what the scripture says, "They divided my clothes among themselves, and for my clothing they cast lots." And that is what the soldiers did. Meanwhile, standing near the cross of Jesus were his mother, and his mother's sister, Mary the wife of Clopas, and Mary Magdalene. When Jesus saw his mother and the disciple whom he loved standing beside her, he said to his mother, "Woman, here is your son." Then he said to the disciple, "Here is your mother." And from that hour the disciple took her into his own home. After this, when Jesus knew that all was now finished, he said (in order to fulfill the scripture), "I am thirsty." A jar full of sour wine was standing there. So they put a sponge full of the wine on a branch of hyssop and held it to his mouth. When Jesus had received the wine, he said, "It is finished." Then he bowed his head and gave up his spirit. Since it was the day of Preparation, the Jews did not want the bodies left on the cross during the Sabbath, especially because that Sabbath was a day of great solemnity. So they asked Pilate to have the legs of the crucified men broken and the bodies removed. Then the soldiers came and broke the legs of the first and of the other who had been crucified with him. But when they came to Jesus and saw that he was already dead, they did not break his legs. Instead, one of the soldiers pierced his side with a spear, and at once blood and water came out. (He who saw this has testified so that you also may believe. His testimony is true, and he knows that he tells the truth.) These things occurred so that the scripture might be fulfilled, "None of his bones shall be broken." And again another passage of scripture says, "They will look on the one whom they have pierced." After these things, Joseph of Arimathea, who was a disciple of Jesus, though a secret one because of his fear of the Jews, asked Pilate to let him take away the body of Jesus. Pilate gave him permission; so he came and removed his body. Nicodemus, who had at first come to Jesus by night, also came, bringing a mixture of myrrh and aloes, weighing about a hundred pounds. They took the body of Jesus and wrapped it with the spices in linen cloths, according to the burial custom of the Jews. Now there was a garden in the place where he was crucified, and in the garden there was a new tomb in which no one had ever been laid. And so, because it was the Jewish day of Preparation, and the tomb was nearby, they laid Jesus there.

"They shouted…'Not this man, but Barabbas!'" (v. 40). Our scripture reading brings us face-to-face with the most dramatic encounter between two people that earth has ever seen: the encounter between Jesus Christ, God's Son, and Pontius Pilate, a Roman *procurator cum procurator*. The procurator possessed full civil, military, and criminal jurisdiction and was the personal appointee of the emperor and directly responsible to him. So what we have here then is an encounter between God and Rome, between righteousness and iniquity. Right in the midst of this encounter, another personality enters the moment. In all likelihood, this person probably never dreamed that he would have a place in redemptive history and we can be equally certain that he never expected to win a popularity contest against someone else. This man is the epitome of Andy Warhol's fifteen minutes of fame. He steps into the picture like a bolt of lightning out of nowhere and disappears just as quickly into obscurity, never to be heard from again. I have imagined that he may well have lived out the rest of his life and died without ever fully understanding what happened that day. Where he came from and where he went afterward, no one knows. This man's name is Barabbas. "They shouted in reply, 'Not this man, but Barabbas!' Now Barabbas was a bandit" (v. 40).

Barabbas's Moniker

Barabbas is a name of Aramaic origin. Aramaic is the language that came into being after the captivity of the

Israelites when the language of the Syrian captors became entangled with the Hebrew language of old Israel. It could be compared to Spanglish, an intermingling of English and Spanish that has evolved in parts of southern Florida and some of the Mexican border regions of the western states. In the Hebrew language the word *ben* means "son." So in Genesis 35:18 we read that as Rachel's soul was departing after a hard labor delivery, she named her about-to-be-born son "Ben-oni, which means 'son of my great sorrow.' Jacob, however, chose another name, Benjamin, meaning 'son of my right hand.' "

In Aramaic, the word for son is not "ben" but *bar.* Perhaps you recall that Simon Peter's real name was Simon Barjonah, or "Simon, son of John." Another example is Bartholomew, meaning "son of Talmei." Now the name is Barabbas. Perhaps your mind is already recognizing what it means. Paul writes, "All who are led by the Spirit of God are sons of God. For you did not receive the spirit of slavery to fall back into fear, but you have received the Spirit of adoption as sons, by whom we cry, 'Abba! Father!' " (Romans 8:14-15 ESV). Ah, *bar* means "son" and *abba* means "father," so Barabbas is the "son of a father."

Actually, many Bible scholars and linguists tell us that Paul's writing at this point is a bit less formal than we usually read. They say that *abba* is a warm, intimate name that might actually be better translated "daddy." Now we are talking about the son-of-a-daddy, Barabbas. It could mean that here was one who was welcomed warmly into a loving family and they named him as they did, "daddy's boy." It would seem, however, that this daddy's boy had taken a wrong turn for now he is "a notorious prisoner," Matthew's gospel tells us (Matthew 27:16). Then again, there is a kind of generic ring to this name Barabbas, for everyone is the son of a daddy or the daughter of a daddy. If this is true, then perhaps we can say that Barabbas stands in this place at this moment in history for each one of us.

Barabbas's Moment

It is perhaps six o'clock in the morning. The top of the temple is beginning to pick up the first light of a new day and it shines out of the night as a new day was dawning. The valley below the Dead Sea still remains dead in darkness because night passes away more slowly in the valley. The narrow city streets remain dark too. However, if you listen closely you can hear footsteps. People are beginning to move. On one dark street, there is a knock on a door. Someone answers and receives a whispered message, "They have taken the Nazarene. He was condemned last night by the Sanhedrin. Perhaps this will be the day that we will see his mighty power arise to destroy Rome!" With that, first one, then two, three, four, and soon a small trickle, then a stream, and soon a vast flowing river of humanity begins to pour from the Passover packed city of Jerusalem toward the palace where Pontius Pilate metes out his Roman justice.

Inside that palace is one unhappy man. Pilate is none too pleased about being awakened in the middle of the night to deal with what he considers essentially a Jewish problem. Yes, the Jews! Pilate's hatred for the Jews is legendary and is matched only by their hatred for him. Gruffly, Pilate steps out and asks the Jews a question, "What accusation do you bring against this man?" (v. 29). In their best ecclesiastical voices, they answer, "If this man were not a criminal, we would not have handed him over to you" (v. 30). Then Pilate responds, "Take him yourselves and judge him according to your law." The Jews reply, "We are not permitted to put anyone to death" (v. 31).

If Pontius Pilate is a master of anything it is the art of political power plays. Matthew helps us with more details again. He reports that an aide comes to see Pilate and whispers a message from Pilate's wife that he should not harm the Nazarene, whom she calls an "innocent man" for she had "suffered a great deal because of a dream about him" (Matthew 27:19).

> So Pilate goes back inside and calls for Jesus to be brought to him. He asks Jesus, "Are you the King of the Jews?" Jesus answered, "Do you ask this on your own, or did others tell you about me?" Pilate replied, "I am not a Jew, am I? Your own nation and the chief priests have handed you over to me. What have you done?" Jesus answered, "My kingdom is not from this world. If my kingdom were from this world, my followers would be fighting to keep me from being handed over to the Jews. But as it is, my kingdom is not from here." Pilate asked him, "So you are a king?" Jesus answered, "You say that I am a king. For this I was born, and for this I came into the world, to testify to the truth. Everyone who belongs to the truth listens to my voice." Pilate asked him, "What is truth?" After he had said this, he went out to the Jews again and told them, "I find no case against him. But you have a custom that I release someone for you at the Passover. Do you want me to release for you the King of the Jews?" They shout in reply, "Not this man, but Barabbas!"
> (vv. 33-40)

Pilate has never seen anything like this before. He remembers the reports from only a few days before that many of the very same people now calling for Barabbas were waving palm branches at this Jesus and shouting hosannas. In calling for Barabbas to be offered against Jesus, he is calling for a notorious criminal. No doubt Pilate reasons that these Jewish leaders and those who follow them would choose Jesus over Barabbas, and he would have pulled off another slick political move and his problem would go away. He imagines that he and his cronies would laugh at this later. "Good old Pilate," they would say, "you played them like a Roman fiddle." But it was not to be, for they cried out with one loud voice, choosing a criminal over the Christ. They choose the son of a father over the Son of the Father and the world would never be the same again.

Barabbas Emancipated

When Pilate heard these words, he brought Jesus outside and sat on the judge's bench at a place called The Stone Pavement, or in Hebrew Gabbatha. Now it was the day of Preparation for the Passover; and it was about noon. He said to the Jews, "Here is your King!" They cried out, "Away with him! Away with him! Crucify him!" Pilate asked them, "Shall I crucify your King?" The chief priests answered, "We have no king but the emperor." Then he handed him over to them to be crucified. So they took Jesus; and carrying the cross by himself, he went out to what is called The Place of the Skull, which in Hebrew is called Golgotha. There they crucified him.
(vv. 13-18)

And Barabbas? Barabbas went free and disappeared.

Or did he? Barabbas... Barabbas! Do you hear me, Barabbas? Are you listening to me, Barabbas? I see you Barabbas... because, my friend, you are Barabbas! And, I am Barabbas! We all have a little bit of Barabbas in us, for we are all guilty of some crime against God, some sin that separated us from our maker. While we may not know what life looks like from the wrong side of a prison cell, the fact is that we are, many of us, still prisoners, trapped by whatever it is that keeps us from absolute surrender to Jesus. Like Barabbas, we may hide but we will not get out of this world alive.

Listen to me, son or daughter of a father, my only hope and your only hope, the only hope of any Barabbas is to realize that another, the sinless Son of the Father, has died in the place of the sinful sons and daughters of all this world's fathers. Having realized this, let us not escape. Instead, let us come clean with Jesus and embrace his grace offered to us through calvary's cross.

103

Easter Sunday
John 20:1-18

Oh Say, Can You See
By the Dawn's Early Light?

Early on the first day of the week, while it was still dark, Mary Magdalene came to the tomb and saw that the stone had been removed from the tomb. So she ran and went to Simon Peter and the other disciple, the one whom Jesus loved, and said to them, "They have taken the Lord out of the tomb, and we do not know where they have laid him." Then Peter and the other disciple set out and went toward the tomb. The two were running together, but the other disciple outran Peter and reached the tomb first. He bent down to look in and saw the linen wrappings lying there, but he did not go in. Then Simon Peter came, following him, and went into the tomb. He saw the linen wrappings lying there, and the cloth that had been on Jesus' head, not lying with the linen wrappings but rolled up in a place by itself. Then the other disciple, who reached the tomb first, also went in, and he saw and believed; for as yet they did not understand the scripture, that he must rise from the dead. Then the disciples returned to their homes. But Mary stood weeping outside the tomb. As she wept, she bent over to look into the tomb; and she saw two angels in white, sitting where the body of Jesus had been lying, one at the head and the other at the feet. They said to her, "Woman, why are you weeping?" She said to them, "They have taken away my Lord, and I do not know where they have laid him." When she had said this, she turned around and saw Jesus standing there, but she did not know that it was Jesus. Jesus said to her, "Woman, why are you weeping? Whom are you looking for?" Supposing him to be the gardener, she said to him, "Sir, if you have carried him away, tell me where you have laid him, and I will take him away." Jesus said to her, "Mary!" She turned and said to him in Hebrew, "Rabboni!" (which means Teacher). Jesus said to her, "Do not hold on to me, because I have not yet ascended to the Father. But go to my brothers and say to them, 'I am ascending to my Father and your Father, to my God and your God.' " Mary Magdalene went and announced to the disciples, "I have seen the Lord"; and she told them that he had said these things to her.

Across the street from the walls that surround the city of David there is a tomb. It looks like any other ancient tomb in that area. Step inside and you will quickly realize that this tomb is different. Someone of status and wealth once owned this tomb. You can tell that it belonged to a person of means because this is a double tomb with two side-by-side burial spaces. What is more, this tomb once contained a body but now it lies empty. The evidence of its having been used is seen in the way that the sides of one of the two grave spaces are cut clean and square, just as they would be if a dead person had once occupied that place. You see, the custom in old Jerusalem was to cut a grave place only roughly ("rough it in," we might say) until the person to be buried there died. When the person died, a gravedigger would then hurriedly cut the grave precisely to the right size. This tomb is different from any other tomb in the world. This is the Garden Tomb, the place many scholars believe Christ's body was laid after his crucifixion. Lives are made livelier inside that tomb, even today. I invite you to come now to that tomb for a while and see with me, through the eyes of faith, some things that were seen there on the first Easter morning.

First, please note that sometimes what we see is not accurate. This was Mary's problem that first Easter:

> Early on the first day of the week, while it was still dark, Mary Magdalene came to the tomb and saw that the stone had been removed from the tomb. So she ran and went to Simon Peter and the other disciple, the one whom Jesus loved, and said to them, "They have taken the Lord out of the tomb, and we do not know where they have laid him."
> (vv. 1-2)

A newspaper report tells of the growing phenomenon of vandals disturbing gravestones in local cemeteries in some American cities. Last Easter, news reports told how some loved ones discovered the removed and broken headstones when they arrived at the cemetery to place Easter flowers on gravesites. Having conducted many funeral services, I have a particular interest in that report and in the accompanying camera footage of turned-over headstones and flower vases. Remembering the grief of bereaved family members and friends I have tried to console at gravesides brings anger to my heart. We can all easily imagine how hurtful it must be to come to the grave of a loved one and find that someone has maliciously disturbed what many would consider to be sacred space. Mary Magdalene's reaction is very understandable when we think about her experience in that context. It is easier to appreciate when we realize that grave robbing was not an uncommon occurrence in Mary's day. We can see how her mind raced to the conclusion that grave robbers had tampered with Jesus' grave. "She ran and went to Simon Peter and the other disciple, the one whom Jesus loved, and said to them, 'They have taken the Lord out of the tomb, and we do not know where they have laid him' " (v. 2).

Mary is upset, hurt, and angry that this has happened to someone she loved. We would be too. Mary, however, rushes to judgment and, as a result, reaches the wrong conclusions. We might do that also were we in her place that morning. She blames her imaginary grave robbers. In short, Mary, though her heart was pure, sees the wrong things. She demonstrates what can happen when we come to Easter with a limited vision.

In God's providential love, the scriptures tell us that Mary does see the risen Lord. Nonetheless, for a moment in time her vision is hampered because she looks with only the partial eyes of what she can see. Therefore, she is blinded by her own presuppositions. She does not expect to see him and she does not! Paul cautions us, "We look not at what can be seen but at what cannot be seen; for what can be seen is temporary, but what cannot be seen is eternal" (2 Corinthians 4:18).

John's thoughts run in the wrong direction at first as well. Scripture records that Peter and John, "the other disciple, the one whom Jesus loved" (v. 2), run to the tomb to substantiate Mary's report. John arrives first. Looking inside he observes "the linen wrappings lying there, but he did not go in" (v. 5). John apparently concludes Mary is right. From where he and stands and looks he sees nothing that leads him to doubt Mary's conclusions concerning this desecration.

It is only when impetuous Peter arrives moments after cautious John and goes right inside the tomb, that the picture begins to come clear. By stepping all the way in, Peter sees the Easter difference as a neatly folded head burial cloth. That cloth testifies that this is no hasty grave robbery.

John finally musters up the courage to step into the empty tomb. When he does, his life changes forever: "He saw and believed" (v. 8). What makes the difference for John? Actually, we could first ask ourselves if there really is any difference for John. What is it that he "believed"? We might conclude that he simply believes Mary's original account. He too concludes that someone has vandalized Jesus' grave.

Two pieces of evidence, however, argue against this: The first is that John already seems to believe Mary's account, for when he arrives at the graveside he can see the stone rolled away and the strips of linen. The second evidence is the scripture verse that follows: "for as yet they did not understand the scripture, that he must rise from the dead" (v. 9). These words were inserted where they are in the text for a purpose. In this case it is so that you and I can "see," that is, that we can understand more fully why Mary and John, and perhaps even Peter, first conclude this is a grave disruption. In short, the idea of the resurrection of Jesus is a totally unexpected event for them. I suggest another possibility that John sees and believes Jesus is alive and John's life changes forever.

What does John see? He sees what he could not see from the door. He sees what only Peter has seen until this moment; he sees, "The cloth that had been on Jesus' head, not lying with the linen wrappings but rolled up in a place by itself" (v. 7). It is a tiny detail, but it tells John everything he needs to know for now and forever. You see, vandals are not generally in the habit of taking care of details. The usual way of hooligans is to rush in, do the dirty deed, and rush out again. It would not be like a grave robber to enter a grave, remove the head cloth from a body, steal the body, and then neatly fold the linen up beside the grave. However, a resurrected Lord might do that!

A risen Lord would very possibly awaken from death, as you and I would arise from sleep. He would sit up calmly, perhaps stretch himself for a moment, take off the cloth that covered his head and face, and fold it neatly before placing it beside the place where he had been lying just minutes before.

How does John see? No one can see the true reality of Christ all alone. It requires a touch from heaven. John sees in the power of God's Holy Spirit. That touch from the Spirit that first comes to John on the resurrection morning to nudge him to step inside the grave touches him once again as he peers at the neatly folded cloth that is there. John demonstrates that no one can stand in the semi-darkness and see the full light of the resurrection. No one can stand on the edge and experience the living Christ. We cannot step up close to Christ and know the fullness of his resurrection power in this life he invites us to live. You must step right into the bowels of the tomb and into the fullness of new life in Christ, before exciting things begin to happen in your life. John's life would never be the same again, nor would he want it to be. No one ever wants to go back to the old life after being touched by the Spirit of the living Christ.

The second point I would make is that this principle is still true. To know resurrection power today, to experience the power of a life transformed, we must be ready to go in deeper than we have ever gone before with Christ. For some of us, this will mean going in deeper with Jesus than we ever planned. We must be willing to go all the way with Jesus. John's life takes on new meaning because he steps into a place that he hesitated to go earlier.

We too must step in all the way with Jesus to really see the difference. As a pastor — as any pastor — can say, with regret: Some of this world's most unhappy people in the church of the resurrected Jesus are those who spend their lives standing on the edges. They are neither out nor are they in. They remind me of the people Dwight L. Moody once described as having, "Just enough religion to make themselves miserable; they cannot be happy at a wild party and they are uncomfortable at a prayer meeting." They bring back memories of that children's song about the Grand Old Duke of York, do you remember?

> The Grand old Duke of York
> He had ten thousand men
> He marched them up to the top of the hill
> And he marched them down again.
> When they were up, they were up
> And when they were down, they were down
> And when they were only halfway up
> They were neither up nor down.

It is the truth! Religion — even Christianity — can make a person desperately unhappy. There are people who claim membership in the church who are always too ready to believe the worst, always too willing to criticize what others do. The truth is that they have not yet stepped inside new life in Christ. They are holding back on going all the way with the Lord of the cross. They have a religion. What they really need is not religion but a relationship with the living Christ. Until they have that relationship, they will live their lives in self-imposed misery of uncertainty and insecurity. I believe it is possible for any one of us to be in this position. Most people who stand on the edge of absolute surrender do so for three primary reasons.

The first is that they do not know what it means to step inside all the way with Christ. Amazing as it may seem, many people are still hung up on the idea that to really get close to Jesus means one has to become a little eccentric about Christ and his church. Unfortunately, some people have been exposed to well-intended Christians who acted just this way. Such would-be super saints come across as being a little bit crazy. Others have met Christians possessed of negative, killjoy spirits, people whose whole talk about faith is full of "thou shalt not!" Observing such people go through life with long faces and negative ways does not encourage others to come to Christ. Unbelievers who witness this form of religion (for it is religion and not the relationship we are called to in Jesus) avoid like a plague really making a commitment to Christ. Truthfully, I can understand why people whose primary exposure to Christianity falls into this category would stand out on the edges of the church. Some of us need to learn that negative news and negative attitudes simply do not draw people to anything, not even Christ. This is not the Christianity of the resurrection or of the Bible. The resurrection that we celebrate this day is the best news that the world will ever hear. Tell it with compassion and enthusiasm wherever you go, Christian!

Another reason some people stand on the edge of commitment to Christ and his church is that they believe they are not good enough for God. They think, "I am not virtuous enough to come close to the Savior, therefore I dare not

111

come." There are many such people all around us. They are right! None of us is good enough. However, they are wrong, because they have an inaccurate view of faith in Christ Jesus. The very reason Jesus died was that we are not good enough. He died in our place to make us good enough through his own goodness. So we must come to him not on our own merits but on his merits alone. He is not expecting us to reach perfection before we become disciples. All he asks is that we come saying, "Dear Lord, I'm not good enough and I have made a lot of mistakes but I am willing to try. I'll probably fail many times but I believe you make up for all my failures."

Yet others stand on the edge of faith because they are not willing to give up control. They have self-made plans and goals that are not yet realized. Their intention is not to be against God and they do intend to follow Christ one day. They say something like, "One day, when I have done everything I plan to do, I will become a Christian. Right now, I just have other priorities." The trouble with this viewpoint is that future planned-for day of commitment may not come. Today is the only day we are guaranteed. Tomorrow may not come for any of us. That is why today is the best day to decide to step in all the way with Jesus. The Bible says, "Now is the acceptable time; see, now is the day of salvation!" (2 Corinthians 6:2). And the Holy Spirit says, "Today, if you hear his voice, do not harden your hearts" (Hebrews 3:7-8). The Bible never speaks about making a faith commitment tomorrow. It always speaks with urgency about today!

In the name of Christ, the risen Lord of the tomb, I speak about going in all the way; about total commitment; about really stepping into absolute surrender of everything we are, and have, and ever hope to be, to God the Father, and to his Son, Jesus.

It is too easy to live life on the edge with reserved commitment but it is never smart. Even Peter tried that at one point. In another chapter John's gospel records that when Christ, after his resurrection, calls again to the once-brash Peter, the big fisherman, having failed Christ is hesitant about making a renewed commitment. Upon seeing John, Peter asks Jesus, "Lord, what about him?" (John 21:21). Peter's question is designed to allow him to give less than his personal best to Christ. Perhaps it seems to Peter that John, following from a distance, might be required to carry less responsibility. He asks it in the context of John following from behind. The Lord responds, "What is that to you? Follow me!" (John 21:22). It is Peter's attempt to excuse himself on the perceived lesser commitment of another, and Christ calls it for what it is. We dare not measure our level of commitment with the adjudged level of someone else's. There is only one against whom we measure our commitment level and that is the Lord Christ himself.

One man, asked to serve on a church board, tried to dodge the responsibility that comes with such a position. He said to his pastor, "Let someone else do it. I don't want to be tied down." "Why not?" his pastor asked. Then the pastor added, "Jesus wasn't tied down. He was nailed down! If he did that for you, how can you ever imagine responding with a short-measure commitment of any kind?"

The fact is we are either inside or outside when it comes to our relationship with Jesus Christ. We are either with him or away from him. John could not stand back and experience the power of the empty tomb. He has to step inside for himself, as must we. Peter could not follow from a distance and become all that Jesus has in mind for him to be. The only way to experience the fullness of resurrection power is to commit to going all the way with Jesus. John stepped in "and believed."

This principal of commitment applies to other areas of life too. Do you know the secret to a contented marriage? It is to take the plunge all the way. Step in with heart and soul, and you will never regret it. It is the same on your job. A sign on a business office wall says, "If you don't believe the dead can come alive again come back at quitting time!" The sign was hung to evoke humor and it does. However, in other places a sign like that may indeed be an accurate measure of the level of dedication some employees bring to work each day. No one ever finds contentment in a job done with half a heart. Only when we give ourselves with enthusiasm do we experience joy in life.

Oh say, can you see by the dawn's early light? It is Resurrection Sunday and all around the world Christians are singing glad hymns of praise to the living Jesus. In your heart (and not just with your lips) are you joining the glorious chorus? Do you have the confidence that Christ alone can bring into our lives? Have you stepped all the way in with Christ? If you have not, then there is no better morning than Easter, and there is no better place than here to come to Jesus all the way. If you are ready to do that, then welcome glad morning. You can see! You can see! You can see! And you will see and believe more!

Easter 2
John 20:19-31

Afraid of Hope!

When it was evening on that day, the first day of the week, and the doors of the house where the disciples had met were locked for fear of the Jews, Jesus came and stood among them and said, "Peace be with you." After he said this, he showed them his hands and his side. Then the disciples rejoiced when they saw the Lord. Jesus said to them again, "Peace be with you. As the Father has sent me, so I send you." When he had said this, he breathed on them and said to them, "Receive the Holy Spirit. If you forgive the sins of any, they are forgiven them; if you retain the sins of any, they are retained." But Thomas (who was called the Twin), one of the twelve, was not with them when Jesus came. So the other disciples told him, "We have seen the Lord." But he said to them, "Unless I see the mark of the nails in his hands, and put my finger in the mark of the nails and my hand in his side, I will not believe." A week later his disciples were again in the house, and Thomas was with them. Although the doors were shut, Jesus came and stood among them and said, "Peace be with you." Then he said to Thomas, "Put your finger here and see my hands. Reach out your hand and put it in my side. Do not doubt but believe." Thomas answered him, "My Lord and my God!" Jesus said to him, "Have you believed because you have seen me? Blessed are those who have not seen and yet have come to believe." Now Jesus did many other signs in the presence of his disciples, which are not written in this book. But these are written so that you may come to believe that Jesus is the Messiah, the Son of God, and that through believing you may have life in his name.

As Harry Houdini, the Budapest born American by adoption stunt performer who is best remembered for his sensational escape acts, lay dying in November 1926, he made a deathbed pact with his wife Bess. He told Bess that he would try to reach her from the other world. For ten years, Bess kept a candle burning below Harry's picture in their home. Each year on the anniversary of his death, Bess gathered in some friends and held a séance hoping she would hear from her late husband. Needless to say, she never once heard a word from him. In 1936, she snuffed out the candle and declared, "That's it! Death is the end. There is nothing more. I now know that for sure because my Harry didn't speak."

Death's Darkness

If you miss church you can miss amazing things! Disciple Thomas missed meeting with Christ's people and as a result he was, in some ways, like Mrs. Houdini. After the crucifixion of Jesus, Thomas sat cheerless, lifeless, hopeless, downspirited, and helpless as he gazed into death's darkness. Jesus was gone. Thomas witnessed it firsthand. What's more, it was the talk of Jerusalem on that Friday afternoon when the sky's darkness blanketed the earth. For Thomas, Jesus was no more. His master was dead! Kaput! Lifeless! Deceased! Finished! Thomas did not meet with the other disciples when they kept the Lord's command to keep on meeting, even as we do each Sunday that we might encourage each other in the faith Jesus gives us.

Why did Thomas not meet? We can merely speculate but it seems that a good guess would be that Thomas reasoned, "What's the use? He is gone." Whatever it was, Thomas was convinced that Jesus was dead — never to live again. Thomas was afflicted with that ultimate, indescribable despair that sees no benefits in tomorrow.

It was not the first time that Thomas stood alone from the other disciples. In John 11:1-54, when Jesus, despite imminent danger at the hands of hostile Jews, declared his intention of going to Bethany to heal Lazarus, Thomas alone opposed the other disciples who sought to dissuade him. "Thomas, who was called the Twin, said to his fellow disciples, 'Let us also go, that we may die with him' " (John 11:16). On the eve of the passion, it was Thomas who led off the discussion with that now well-known question, "Lord, we do not know where you are going. How can we know the way?" (John 14:5). Jesus spoke directly to Thomas with an answer that has directed Christians and new converts for 2,000 years now: Jesus said to him, "I am the way, and the truth, and the life. No one comes to the Father except through me. If you know me, you will know my Father also. From now on you do know him and have seen him" (John 14:6-7). Thomas, more than any of the other disciples, had an enquiring mind.

When the others went to Thomas and said, "We have seen the Lord!" (v. 25), Thomas, ever the doubter, could only mutter, "That may be good enough for you but I will not be drawn into your emotion-laden fantasy. Dead people do not rise!" His actual answer — crude, rude, gory, unbelieving — set a materialistic three-step test: He said to them, "Unless I see the mark of the nails in his hands (step 1), put my finger in the mark of the nails (step 2), and my hand in his side (step 3), I will not believe" (v. 25). Please understand, Thomas was no atheist. He was a momentary agnostic. He was, I suspect, thinking, "I saw Jesus' body, lifeless and limp, on that cross. I watched him buried in a tomb. I saw the stone rolled across the opening. I just cannot believe it. Dead people do not rise!" He was afraid to hope that Jesus had defeated death. So Thomas sits in the hall of human history cheerless and gazing into the darkness, his name synonymous with doubt for two millennia, because for that moment in time he refused to believe in the possibility of the resurrection of the Lord of glory. For Thomas, Jesus was over and his wonderful promises ended up on a rough Roman cross.

Dear friends, can you see that doubt, unbelief, and negativity never make us better? You will never see a monument to a doubter. No doubter ever built a successful business, found a cure for disease, conquered depression, or motivated

117

people to rise above their circumstances and take hold of life. If you want to live a victorious Christian life you must stay away from negative people. "Doubting Thomas," we call him; just "Doubting Thomas."

Doubt and negativity! They are everywhere around us. Some of us may be waiting for a pathology report on a loved one or ourselves. Perhaps some of us are wondering if we are going to make it financially. Others may be wondering if our marriages will survive, or perhaps if the marriages of our children will endure. These are all real concerns, but I must tell you that we will not find the answers or any comfort if we wrap ourselves in doubt and negativity.

A pastor friend of mine was called to a large city church that experienced a rapid turnover of pastors. He was not there long when he encountered Peggy who called herself the "church mother." Peggy led a series of Bible studies in the church and from that platform, she cast doubt on successive pastors and the programs they promoted. Finally my friend saw no way to deal with this situation other than to confront Peggy about what she was doing. She received his caution with great anger and threatened to leave the church. Soon after that she did leave. When word of her leaving reached the members of Peggy's Bible studies, some of them wondered if the church would survive without her. It was not long before they saw that not only could the church survive; it actually began to thrive and grow. Peggy never realized that the seeds of doubt and negativity do not produce a healthy harvest.

Apparently somewhere in the context of that first conversation with the other disciples, or perhaps in a follow-up conversation, Thomas the doubter was persuaded that he had nothing to lose if he met with the other ten (remember Judas the betrayer was dead by now) one more time the following Sunday. When the first day of the new week came, Thomas was there among the other remaining disciples. The group locked the door. Suddenly there was an epiphany, a visitation from heaven filled with ecstasy and unbelievable delight. But there was also a confrontation. For the Lord, who the Psalmist reminds us in Psalm 139, hears every word before we say it, had heard what Thomas said. The resurrected Jesus turned Thomas' crude three-step test back on him: "Put your finger here and see my hands. Reach out your hand and put it in my side. Do not doubt but believe" (v. 27). Can you imagine the embarrassment and the shame that Thomas must have felt there before them all? Interestingly, there is no record that Thomas did what Jesus gave him permission to do. Seeing the risen wounded Lord was sufficient for Thomas. Jesus responded, "Have you believed because you have seen (notice, not 'touched') me? Blessed are those who have not seen and yet have come to believe" (vv. 29-30). There is not a page in the Bible that has a good place for unbelief or despair in life.

Life's Light

What I just said about doubt is true for all our lives! Unbelief, lack of faith, and despair never make us better. This doubt never makes a home better. It can make it bitter for all who live there. It never makes a church, business, or educational program better. Search the world over and you'll never find any great lasting thing that was born out of unbelief, faithlessness, and unwillingness to trust. Don't you know that when Thomas heard those words of his falling from lips of the risen Jesus, it surely must have crushed the doubter? I can imagine that he felt ashamed and that in his shame his dark deadness turned to life's light. He found the will to repent and confess, "My Lord and my God" (v. 28). Thomas surely would never again allow doubt to drive his way through life.

Those words, "My Lord and my God," mark the great pinnacle point of human declaration in John's gospel! They mark the turning point in the life of Thomas. In that moment when Thomas saw that indeed Jesus was raised from the dead, he also saw something of what that would mean for the rest of his life. That affirmation becomes the turning point in anyone's life who utters those words because no one can look at the resurrected Lord of calvary's cross and be the same again. For Thomas, life would never be the same again. Thomas ultimately became a martyr for his faith. As Jesus laid down his life for Thomas, so one day Thomas would lay down his life for Jesus and the gospel.

Christian tradition holds that in 52 AD, Thomas arrived in Kerala to begin the establishment of the Christian church in India. He preached faithfully for twenty years and established seven churches before he was speared to death for preaching the gospel in December 72 AD. Today, you can visit San Thome Basilica in the city of Chennai (sometimes called Madras) in India. That church is believed to stand on the very spot where Thomas shed his life's blood rather than deny his Lord and God.

Blind Bliss!

Jesus said to Thomas, "Have you believed because you have seen me? Blessed are those who have not seen and yet have come to believe" (v. 29).

Thomas once believed that seeing was believing, but Jesus teaches us that believing is seeing. Michael May was blinded when he was only three years of age and for the next 42 years he lived his life in total darkness. Then, when he was 45, he was given the possibility of seeing again through a revolutionary transplant surgery. Before Michael's sight was restored perhaps only 40 people had experienced new sight and some with mixed degrees of success. For many of them, moving from a world of total darkness to a world of color and light involved a major learning curve. Before their surgeries, they did not need to understand concepts of height or depth or three-dimensional shapes. Nor could they read facial expressions or body language. Often family members could not understand this. They also needed to learn that the change often took time. Michael's case was different. As his surgeon finally removed the bandages from his eyes, just like the other patients, Michael could not identify distance or height or the other things prior patients could not identify. The difference, however, was this: Michael refused to be discouraged. He entered his new world of sight with a spirit of a child going on a great adventure. Like a child, he peppered the people around him with questions. "What is that?" Is that a tree? Is this a flower? Is that a car? May I touch it? Like a child, nothing excited Michael more than riding a hotel elevator and he rode it up and down repeatedly. He played ball games and Frisbee with his son, missing a lot before he got the hang of what was happening and was able to coordinate sight and hand. Things that sighted people assumed, Michael thought of as all part of his adventure — like a speeding car or motorcycle — and that the leap of new sight was not really adventuresome if everything felt safe. As a result, every day had its mixtures of success and failure, but most important this constant stream of new opportunities to see and experience allowed Michael to grow and change for the better.

The same is true when we come to Jesus. We will see all of life with new eyes. Paul writes,

> I pray that the God of our Lord Jesus Christ, the Father of glory, may give you a spirit of wisdom and revelation as you come to know him, so that, with the eyes of your heart enlightened, you may know what is the hope to which he has called you, what are the riches of his glorious inheritance among the saints. (Ephesians 1:17-18)

Thomas did not know resurrection hope because he was afraid to hope.

Who can blame Thomas? We have all experienced our moments of unbelief because of doubt. There have been times in all our lives when we were afraid to hope.

Let me tell you about the fear of hope. It stands against everything Jesus taught. It prefers ignorance and death over light. It hinders growth in people everywhere; even people in the church. Many well-intentioned modern-day Thomases unwittingly give too much space to doubt and darkness. Living with too many old memories, such church members believe bad news over good news. Many church people are even now held hostage by old hurt, disappointment, prejudice, hatred, cynicism, doubt, fear, ignorance, low expectations, hostility, and tension. Their song of faith goes something like this:

> Backward Christian soldiers
> Fleeing from the light,
> With the cross of Jesus often out of sight
> Christ our rightful Master stands against the foe
> Yet, forward to the future we're afraid to go!
>
> Crowns and thrones may perish,
> Kingdoms rise and wane,
> But our cross of Jesus, hidden will remain.
> Gates of hell should never, 'gainst the church prevail,
> We have Christ's own promise, but we're scared we'll fail.
>
> Sit still then, ye people;
> Join our useless throng.
> Blend with ours your voices
> In our feeble song.
>
> Blessings, ease, and comfort
> Ask from Christ the King
> With our kind of thinking,
> We won't do a thing!

Call it what it really is: S-I-N! In the name of Jesus Christ the Lord over the cross, come away from that kind of thinking and believe the good news: Jesus lives! Thomas believed it could not be and, so for him it would not be. Before you can believe good news you must hope it. Then let hope give way to belief. Act as though the good news is true and it will come true through you.

Thomas had to learn the good news that doubt is not true. Only this is true: Jesus Christ is alive. He is risen and we can face whatever comes our way with the confidence and peace that comes from knowing he lives in us and "we know that all things work together for good for those who love God, who are called according to his purpose" (Romans 8:28). What a wonderful Savior!

Do you see him now? If you do, go out and show him to your world. Live like you have seen him! Talk like you have seen him! Laugh like you have been in his company. We are the resurrection witnesses for this generation! All the rest are disciples of dread darkness and doubt. Only the people of Jesus worship a living Savior with joy unspeakable and full of glory no matter what else happens.

I believe that this unbelieving world is looking for a life that is filled with hope, certainty, and joy. That life is only found in the one who Thomas called "Lord and God." Let this world see from your face that you are one of his. Let them see him through how you live.

And if you have been straddling the fence of doubt and unbelief, then I invite you in his name to get off now and never mount the fence again for Jesus' sake and for the sake of your own soul!

When Heartbreak Turns to Heartburn!

Now on that same day two of them were going to a village called Emmaus, about seven miles from Jerusalem, and talking with each other about all these things that had happened. While they were talking and discussing, Jesus himself came near and went with them, but their eyes were kept from recognizing him. And he said to them, "What are you discussing with each other while you walk along?" They stood still, looking sad. Then one of them, whose name was Cleopas, answered him, "Are you the only stranger in Jerusalem who does not know the things that have taken place there in these days?" He asked them, "What things?" They replied, "The things about Jesus of Nazareth, who was a prophet mighty in deed and word before God and all the people, and how our chief priests and leaders handed him over to be condemned to death and crucified him. But we had hoped that he was the one to redeem Israel. Yes, and besides all this, it is now the third day since these things took place. Moreover, some women of our group astounded us. They were at the tomb early this morning, and when they did not find his body there, they came back and told us that they had indeed seen a vision of angels who said that he was alive. Some of those who were with us went to the tomb and found it just as the women had said; but they did not see him." Then he said to them, "Oh, how foolish you are, and how slow of heart to believe all that the prophets have declared! Was it not necessary that the Messiah should suffer these things and then enter into his glory?" Then beginning with Moses and all the prophets, he interpreted to them the things about himself in all the scriptures. As they came near the village to which they were going, he walked ahead as if he were going on. But they urged him strongly, saying, "Stay with us, because it is almost evening and the day is now nearly over." So he went in to stay with them. When he was at the table with them, he took bread, blessed and broke it, and gave it to them. Then their eyes were opened, and they recognized him; and he vanished from their sight. They said to each other, "Were not our hearts burning within us while he was talking to us on the road, while he was opening the scriptures to us?" That same hour they got up and returned to Jerusalem; and they found the eleven and their companions gathered together. They were saying, "The Lord has risen indeed, and he has appeared to Simon!" Then they told what had happened on the road, and how he had been made known to them in the breaking of the bread.

Here again we find Luke the physician at his best. Although not one of the original twelve, in his own exquisite and unique way this doctor-disciple of Jesus gives us details with clarity indicating that he is close to Jesus and the disciples and can speak with the authority of an eyewitness to the things he tells us. In his opening phrase in the passage, Luke tells us that "two of them were going to a village called Emmaus." Just a few verses earlier in verse 10 of this chapter, Luke indicates that the two are apostles. However, near the end (v. 33) he writes, "That same hour they got up and returned to Jerusalem; and they found the eleven and their companions gathered together." So, we must assume that Luke's use of the term "apostle" is to be understood in a broader sense than merely assuming that it is a pure synonym for the eleven remaining after Judas takes his own life. Three words fit the story. The first of them is doubt.

Doubt!

We read, "They stood still, looking sad" (v. 17). The following statement by one of them, called Cleopas, indicates that they are two devotees of Jesus whom they describe as "a prophet mighty in deed and word before God and all the people and... our chief priests and leaders handed him over to be condemned to death and crucified him" (Luke 24:20). So it is not stretching the facts to say that their hearts are broken. Not only have they lost someone they admired as a true prophet of God; to make matters worse, it was their own chief priests and leaders who caused this travesty of justice to happen. Furthermore, they add, "We had hoped that he was the one to redeem Israel. Yes, and besides all this, it is now the third day since these things took place." Three days! Three long days since hope has been snatched from them! Now, his body is missing and they have no idea of its whereabouts (see v. 21). For these two — as it is even today for many people — the notion that Jesus Christ, God's Son who was crucified on a rough Roman cross and rose on the third day is news too good to be true.

Clearly from their positive evaluation of Jesus' ministry, they have been around him on more than one occasion for they know him as "a prophet mighty in deed and word." Yet doubt's dark clouds have enveloped them and they have forgotten that Jesus preached that he would rise again after three days: "He began to teach them that the Son of Man must undergo great suffering, and be rejected by the elders, the chief priests, and the scribes, and be killed, and after three days rise again. He said all this quite openly" (Mark 8:31-32).

Others have told them: "Moreover, some women of our group astounded us. They were at the tomb early this morning, and when they did not find his body there, they came back and told us that they had indeed seen a vision of angels who said that he was alive. Some of those who were with us went to the tomb and found it just as the women had said; but they did not see him" (vv. 22-24). Yet having heard from Jesus and the women who found the tomb empty, these men, who are on their way to Emmaus, the place whose name means "warm springs," have no good news. Their hearts are broken by their failure to take the word of Jesus along with the word of the disciples who have been to the empty tomb. So blinded are their eyes by doubt that even when Jesus joins them for their walk along that road, they do not recognize him.

Luke tells this story as a lesson for present-day people like us. We can be so caught up in our doubts about faith that we fail to see and hear the obvious. Again and again the Bible tells us that if we look around, we will see evidence of God. Consider, for example, these words, "The heavens declare the glory of God, and the sky above proclaims his handiwork. Day to day pours out speech, and night to night reveals knowledge" (Psalm 19:1-2). Again, Saint Paul writes,

> The wrath of God is revealed from heaven against all ungodliness and unrighteousness of men, who by their unrighteousness suppress the truth. For what can be known about God is plain to them, because God has shown it to them. For his invisible attributes, namely, his eternal power and divine nature, have been clearly perceived, ever since the creation of the world, in the things that have been made. So they are without excuse. (Romans 1:18-20 ESV)

He is saying that all around us there are evidences of God. There is no place for doubt and doubters have no excuse.

As a pastor, I am persuaded that many church people really do not believe in the resurrection of Jesus. If they did, there would never be an empty pew in any church in the land. Some of us, like Zechariah when the angel told him that his barren wife Elizabeth would bear a son who would be John the Baptist, are just happy to bumble our way through life uncertain and unhappy. Moreover, given the choice like these two disciples we meet in today's scripture reading, some church people choose to believe bad news over good news.

Not many years ago, a new highway was under construction somewhere in England. An old vacant and abandoned dilapidated building sat in its pathway. When the wreckers tore it down and cleared off the ground where that building had stood for generations, they found nothing that caught their attention. A few weeks later, however, after that ground was exposed to sunshine and rain, flowers sprung up. No one could identify them. A botanist was called in. He said, "I think I know what it is but I'm afraid to believe it." Soon more botanists came. Someone said, "These are plants the Romans imported to England during their occupation about 2,000 years ago. For a long time we have presumed them extinct." The first botanist said, "That is what I was thinking but I was afraid to believe it!"

Afraid to believe it! For some people, even church people, Jesus Christ, God's Son crucified on a rough Roman cross and rising on the third day is news too good to be believed. Frozen by doubt, they miss the best news the world will ever hear!

Difference!

"Beginning with Moses and all the prophets, he (Jesus) interpreted to them the things about himself in all the scriptures" (v. 27). Scripture does not give us the details, but perhaps he explains who he is to them in words similar to these:

In Genesis I am the seed of the woman.
In Exodus I am the Passover lamb.
In Leviticus I am the high priest.
In Numbers I am the pillar of cloud by day and the pillar of fire by night.
In Deuteronomy I am the prophet like unto Moses.
In Joshua I am the captain of our salvation.
In Judges I am your judge and lawgiver.
In Ruth I am your kinsman redeemer.
In 1 Samuel I am the ark and mercy seat.
In 2 Samuel I am the king declared by the prophets.
In 1 Kings I am the true temple where all God's people gather.
In 2 Kings I am the mighty miracle maker.

In 1 Chronicles I am Adam's descendent who reigns forever.
In 2 Chronicles I am ever protected royalty.
In Ezra I am our faithful scribe.
In Nehemiah I am the rebuilder of broken down walls.
In Esther I am Mordecai.
In Job I am the dayspring from on high.
In Psalms I am the Lord your shepherd.
In Proverbs I am God's word fitly spoken.
In Ecclesiastes I make sense out of nonsense.
In Solomon's song I am the lover and the bridegroom.
In Isaiah I am the holy one of Israel.
In Jeremiah I am the righteous branch.
In Lamentations I am the weeping prophet.
In Ezekiel I am the wonderful four-faced man.
In Daniel I am the fourth man in the burning furnace.
In Hosea I am the forever faithful husband.
In Joel I am the Baptist with the Holy Spirit and fire.
In Amos I am your burden-bearer.
In Obadiah I am mighty to save.
In Jonah I am swallowed up but alive on the third day.
In Micah I am the messenger of beautiful feet.
In Nahum I am the avenger of God's elect.
In Habakkuk I am God's evangelist, crying, "Revive thy work...."
In Zephaniah I am the Savior.
In Haggai I am the restorer of God's lost heritage.
In Zechariah I am the true king rejected by his own people.
In Malachi I am the son of righteousness.

The difference is the second word that jumps at us out of this passage. These two disciples on the way to Emmaus were afraid of change. It is all too easy for us to get stuck in our ruts and we reason that if the resurrection of Jesus really is true, then we must change our way of thinking and living. Indeed, that is exactly true, because no one can honestly examine the resurrection and remain the same. For example, after we believe in the resurrection we can no longer be satisfied to live with our old half-measure commitment to Jesus and his church.

In Isaac Newton's first law of motion, Newton asserts that

everything continues in a state of rest unless it is compelled to change by forces impressed upon it. He is right. Almost everything about this world is in a constant state of flux. Another way of stating the same truth is to say that change is one of life's few constants.

There's an old story about two fellows who lived their whole lives in a large northern city. One day in a conversation about something one of them had read about rural life, they decided they needed to see it for themselves. Together they resolved to sell out and give up city life for good. They would do what the early settlers had done generations before them and live off the land. They would plant their own vegetables and raise their own meat. That would mean they would take the proceeds from what they had sold and buy a farm. Looking in a newspaper, they saw an advertisement saying that a Texas ranch was for sale. They agreed that it looked just like what they would need and bought it sight unseen, except for a single picture in the advertisement. Now that they owned a farm, they would need a truck. So heading out to a dealership on the outskirts of the city, they bought a nice truck. The next morning they got up early and headed for Texas. Arriving at their new ranch, they were very excited. It soon became obvious that they needed a mule. They got in their pickup and went to their nearest neighbor to see if he had a mule he might want to sell. The neighbor said, "I sure don't." Nevertheless, they decided to visit the man for a while; even though he lived about a mile away, he was their nearest neighbor. As they talked with the neighbor, some watermelons that were stacked against the neighbor's barn caught their eye. They had never seen watermelons so large before and curiosity got the best of them. "What are they?" they asked him. By now, the neighboring rancher seeing they were unenlightened city fellows, decided to have some fun at their expense. "Them's mule eggs!" he told them. "Mule eggs?" they exclaimed. "Yup! Take one home and keep it warm. When it hatches you'll have your mule." "Wow!" they exclaimed together, "What a deal, a mule of our own and we can raise it as a baby." Gullible, they bought the biggest one they could see and carefully laid it in the back of their pickup. Soon after that, they headed toward their new home. Along the way, they decided to each take turns sitting up at night in case their mule egg hatched in the middle of the night. However, on the way home they hit a pothole and the watermelon rolled out. It hit the road, bounced, and burst wide open. Seeing what happened in their rearview mirrors, they quickly found a place to turn around and drove back to where it happened. In the meantime, a huge Texas jackrabbit came by and spotted the burst watermelon lying in the middle of the road. He hopped over to it and began to eat. The city fellows drove up a couple of minutes afterward and saw the long-eared jackrabbit sitting in the middle of the road munching on the watermelon. The two new ranchers screamed with delight when they saw those long ears, "Our mule!" As they jumped out of their pickup the scared jackrabbit ran off. The two city fellows followed it in hot pursuit. As jackrabbits do, it first hopped around in a circle. The two men tried to catch it but the faster they ran after it the faster it ran away from them. Finally they were exhausted and could go no further. Winded, they collapsed one on top of the other, each one gasping for breath. After a minute or two, one of them raised himself up on his elbows and declared to his buddy, "Ben, I guess our mule got away." Ben replied, "It's okay, Bob. I'm not sure I want to plow as fast as he can run anyhow!"

We smile at that story because it sounds a bit silly! But think about this: Is it not true for some of us that our single greatest hindrance to really doing business with the resurrected Jesus is that we are just not sure we want to plow that fast anyhow? We want a Jesus who will let us live at our own speed. We do not want to go too hard or too far with him. Yet the truth is we will get no more out of Christian faith than we are prepared to put into it. There is no real joy in half-hearted Christianity that does as little as possible with Jesus and expects very little to happen.

These two men on the way to Emmaus simply are not prepared for God to work in new ways in their little world. As a result, they almost miss the greatest miracle of all time because they are not ready for the possibility of God doing a new and glorious thing.

They are totally amazed to learn that they have walked the seven miles from Jerusalem to Emmaus in the company of the very one they loved, the risen Jesus, whom they had seen and heard many times before. What is it about us that hinders us from experiencing the risen Lord's great surprises?

Decision!

Here is the third word that calls for our attention in this passage. Sooner or later, each of us must decide how we will respond to the resurrection of the Lord Jesus. "They said to each other, 'Were not our hearts burning within us while he was talking to us on the road, while he was opening the scriptures to us?' " (v. 32). Their heartbreak turns to heart-burn! Not the kind of heartburn that calls for Prilosec, but good heartburn. Their hearts, once broken with sadness, now burn with passion for the living Lord of the cross.

Those Emmaus disciples are slow to recognize the truth when they first see him. Perhaps that is because they are walking away from Jerusalem, where the community of Christians met. When they do see Jesus, their lives and their world are positively transformed as never before. What are you prepared to give in return for the risen Christ's calvary love? Do you really believe he rose again from the dead on the third day? To believe that calls for change. "If anyone is in Christ, there is a new creation: everything old has passed away; see, everything has become new!" (2 Corinthians

5:17). Make no mistake; some things have to change when you decide to follow Jesus. Old attitudes and lifestyles have no place in his kingdom and they really cannot have any place with us when we become citizens of it.

In Jesus' name, I invite you to come to the new Jerusalem, the church of the Lord Jesus Christ. Come believing, expecting, and working for wonderful things to happen for you and for those you love. Exchange your broken heart for a heart that burns with a passion for his truth. Wouldn't it be wonderful if tonight, before you go to sleep, you could thank God that your new heart in Jesus began to beat this very day?

The Gate to Grace, Goodness, and Glory

"Very truly, I tell you, anyone who does not enter the sheepfold by the gate but climbs in by another way is a thief and a bandit. The one who enters by the gate is the shepherd of the sheep. The gatekeeper opens the gate for him, and the sheep hear his voice. He calls his own sheep by name and leads them out. When he has brought out all his own, he goes ahead of them, and the sheep follow him because they know his voice. They will not follow a stranger, but they will run from him because they do not know the voice of strangers." Jesus used this figure of speech with them, but they did not understand what he was saying to them. So again Jesus said to them, "Very truly, I tell you, I am the gate for the sheep. All who came before me are thieves and bandits; but the sheep did not listen to them. I am the gate. Whoever enters by me will be saved, and will come in and go out and find pasture. The thief comes only to steal and kill and destroy. I came that they may have life, and have it abundantly."

A pastor friend who lived in an apartment complex in San Francisco tells about the time that he and his wife parked their brand new Honda Accord under cover in the secured parking area next to their apartment complex. The next day they decided to celebrate the purchase of that new car by going out to breakfast together. Not only would they enjoy eating out together, it would give them another opportunity to drive their new automobile. Leaving the apartment building, they greeted the guard on duty at the gate of the parking garage. They walked along a row of parked cars and, he reports, as they walked up to their new Honda they knew right away that something was not right because the passenger side front door was not closed completely. As they drew closer they discovered that the dashboard had been broken, the radio was stolen as well as, believe it or not, the burglar alarm! They called the police and the person who took their report said, "Let me guess, you were parked at that nice apartment complex on Burlington Avenue and your car is a Honda Accord. Am I right?" "Yes," he responded, "do you already know about this?" "No," replied the person on the other end of the telephone, "but you are the eleventh person who has called us this morning from that apartment complex and all of you were parked in that same undercover parking lot and you all own Honda Accords and all of your dashboards are torn up and your radios and burglar alarms stolen."

Can we imagine how violated that couple felt? When they spoke again to the guard at the gate he told of how a guard had been on duty all through the night but the thieves did not enter by the gate. Instead they scaled a fence on the far side of the parking lot and did their work under cover of darkness. Thieves violate the common trust of the neighborhoods and communities they rob. They steal not only car radios or whatever else they choose to take, they also create emotional turmoil for the people in those neighborhoods and communities. Jesus says, "Very truly, I tell you, anyone who does not enter the sheepfold by the gate but climbs in by another way is a thief and a bandit" (v. 1).

Come with me to one of the most moving and inviting chapters in the entire Bible. John chapter 10 is also one of the most beloved passages in all the scriptures. The teaching in this chapter reminds us of some of the parables that Matthew, Mark, and Luke record in their gospels. However, there is one glaring difference and we find it in verse 6 where John calls these words from the Lord's lips a "figure of speech." It is an allegory not a parable. Jesus is not talking about violated cars

136

here but about something far more important and vital. He speaks about sheep and ultimately we realize that he is speaking about people as his sheep. In doing this the way that he does, Jesus shows us the heart of a true shepherd, his heart, and here he sets out anew the mission for all his people. The people who heard this teaching would have understood it well for the image of the shepherd was one with which they were familiar. "The sheep follow him because they know his voice" (v. 4). In the Middle East, unlike the United States and many other parts of the world, the shepherd walks ahead of his sheep and not behind them. As he walks, he talks to the sheep, giving them commands. The sheep may not immediately understand the shepherd's words but they know his voice. It is the voice of tender authority and caring. They have come to learn that he will take them to good pasture and will lead them into safe places. And when the people hear Jesus say, "I am the gate for the sheep" (v. 7), they understand what that means. Now, the imagery shifts.

Our Gate Is a Person

Jesus starts by saying that the shepherd enters by the gate. "The gatekeeper opens the gate for him, and the sheep hear his voice" (v. 3). Now in verse 7, the whole tenor of this figure changes dramatically. Jesus calls himself the gate. This is an image that is as meaningful today as it was when Jesus spoke these words. The Greek word for "I am" is the equivalent to the Hebrew name that God gave himself when he spoke to Moses, who, of course, was also a shepherd. Perhaps you recall that conversation when God commissions Moses to go down to Egypt and call for the release of the children of Israel from the pharaoh's bondage. The scene is the burning bush after God tells Moses to take off his shoes because he is standing on holy ground. Then God introduces himself to Moses from the fire with a name that God uses of himself only one time in scripture; a name that is firmly established in both Judaism and Christianity. That name is "I am." God said, "I am the God of your father, the God of Abraham, the God of Isaac, and the God of Jacob" (Exodus 3:6). Moses, afraid to look at God, hides his face, scripture tells us. After God commissions him, Moses has a question for God, "If I come to the Israelites and say to them, 'The God of your ancestors has sent me to you,' and they ask me, 'What is his name?' what shall I say to them?" God said to Moses, "I AM WHO I AM." He said further, "Thus you shall say to the Israelites, 'I AM has sent me to you' " (Exodus 3:13-14).

Often we stop reading that passage there but what comes next is, if anything, even more important, especially for Christians: "God also said to Moses, 'Thus you shall say to the Israelites, "The Lord, the God of your ancestors, the God of Abraham, the God of Isaac, and the God of Jacob, has sent me to you": This is my name forever, and this my title for all generations' " (Exodus 3:15). Now here is Jesus using that very name for himself, just as he does in each of his "I am" statements. Our gate is a person called Jesus. He is God revealed in human flesh and living among his people.

A pastor was leading a group of people on a Holy Land tour. On an afternoon of free time he went walking through some fields near Bethlehem. As he walked, he met an Arab shepherd, a man — he was to learn — who was not a Christian and who had not read the Bible. Imagining that this man could very well be a direct descendant of those shepherds we have all sung about and who are in all the re-enactments of the Christmas story — the ones who heard the heavenly angels sing of the birth of the Christ Child and who rushed to the Bethlehem manger — the pastor felt a compelling urge to engage the shepherd in conversation. What he learned in the conversation that ensued was that this man was the living embodiment of the lesson we read here. The Arab shepherd was showing off his sheep herd to the pastor and in the course of the conversation pointed out the area where the sheep were penned up each evening. "After I lead my flock in there," he said, pointing to a circular rock fence, "they know they can lie down and sleep in complete safety." The pastor immediately recognized that there was no gate on that sheep pen and asked the shepherd, "Where is your gate?" He was thinking that all he could see was the opening to the sheep pen but he saw nothing that secured the sheep inside the pen. At that point the Arab shepherd turned his thumb toward himself and said, "I am the gate. After my sheep are safely in the pen and they lie down, I lay my body across the opening. The legs of the sheep are too short to be able to step over me and no wolf can get to them without first getting past me."

When Jesus is our gate, we can rest in peace for he assures us that we will be kept safe against anything this world can bring against us. In the Old Testament, the prophet Isaiah put this idea in these words: "No weapon that is fashioned against you shall prosper, and you shall confute every tongue that rises against you in judgment. This is the heritage of the servants of the Lord and their vindication from me, says the Lord" (Isaiah 54:17).

"I am the gate," says Jesus, "whoever enters by me will be saved, and will come in and go out and find pasture" (v. 9). When he says that, Jesus is reaffirming that promise God gives through Isaiah and every other promise of God's provision and protecting care. Let me tell you more about that gate.

Jesus assures us in these words that no one or nothing can get to us without passing by him. The best example of this in scripture is the story of Job. In Job 1:10, Satan recognizes that God has planted a hedge around Job. Satan may attack things around Job but he cannot lay a finger on God's protected servant. The same is true for us. Scripture teaches us that God's eyes run to and fro throughout the whole earth

(2 Chronicles 16:9 ESV); yet, it also teaches us, "Truly the eye of the Lord is on those who fear him, on those who hope in his steadfast love" (Psalm 33:18). God keeps his eye on the whole world all the time. However, at the same time, he keeps a closer, constant microscopic look on his own chosen ones. We are protected and we shall not be stolen. Jesus says,

> My sheep hear my voice. I know them, and they follow me. I give them eternal life, and they will never perish. No one will snatch them out of my hand. What my Father has given me is greater than all else, and no one can snatch it out of the Father's hand.
> (John 10:27-29)

We live under the all-seeing protective hand of the one who loved us all the way to calvary and who loves us still. Our gate is the person of Jesus Christ, God's Son.

There is more here: Jesus is the gate and the gate works two ways. Not only does Jesus, our gate, protect us, he is our gate of admission who opens up the way for us to come to the Father. In fact, we must note that the Bible says he is the only gate to the Father: "I am the way, and the truth, and the life. No one comes to the Father except through me" (John 14:6). So we see that no one can get at God's flock without going through Jesus and no one gets into God's flock without coming through Jesus. "There is salvation in no one else, for there is no other name under heaven given among mortals by which we must be saved" (Acts 4:12).

Think about this: Salvation comes only through Jesus. Baptism cannot make it happen. Religion and ritual cannot do it. Church membership cannot make it happen. Good works cannot make it happen. Following the Ten Commandments cannot make it happen. Only Jesus can make it happen. It can happen only through God's grace in Jesus Christ. Have you been through the gate called Jesus?

140

Our Gate Is a Proposition

Not only is our gate a person, our gate is a proposal. In John 10, Jesus offers a proposition to all who are not yet living for him. Here it is: "Whoever enters by me will be saved" (v. 9). If you have been walking away from Jesus, this is the most amazing offer that you will ever receive. The key is in that word, "Whoever." This is an offer of God's receiving grace to everyone. The church of Jesus Christ is not a society for beautiful, well-connected people. In fact, the only connection we need to receive Christ and join his church is that we acknowledge we are connected to sin; that is, we are sinners. Other societies require prospective members to provide references as to how good they are. Only the church requires an admission that we are not good and that we need a Savior. When we admit that, Jesus makes another commitment. He says, "Anyone who comes to me I will never drive away" (John 6:37).

Remember the gate has a dual purpose. One purpose is to keep danger outside. The other purpose is to let people inside. Jesus makes a proposition that says we can enter. "Whoever enters by me." That is different from saying, "Those I allow to enter" in that it puts the responsibility on entering on "whoever." This is what it means: God offers his salvation but we must demonstrate a willingness to partake of it for it to be effective.

The certainty of this proposition is found in the words "will be saved." "Whoever enters by me will be saved," says Jesus. We note that Jesus does not say that those who enter may be saved, or are sometimes saved, or even, usually are saved. He says they "will be saved." This means that we can accept this proposition and enter this gate called Jesus with confidence.

From what are we saved? We are saved from sin's punishment. That is, no longer will our old sins be held against us. Paul writes, "For the wages of sin is death, but the free

141

gift of God is eternal life in Christ Jesus our Lord" (Romans 6:23). Does the memory of something awful that you did haunt you? Do you fear facing God who knows everything about you, even that thing you wish you had never done? In Jesus, our gateway to God, we have a free gift from God that cannot be bought or earned. In Jesus, you are freely forgiven forever.

From what are we saved? We are saved from sin's power. "For sin will have no dominion over you, since you are not under law but under grace" (Romans 6:14). Do you come from a dysfunctional background? Of course, you do. We all do because there is dysfunctionality in every human life since Adam's fall. Hear now this good news: In Jesus Christ we find the gate of deliverance from that old bondage. In him we get a new start. Paul assures us,

> No testing has overtaken you that is not common to everyone. God is faithful, and he will not let you be tested beyond your strength, but with the testing he will also provide the way out so that you may be able to endure it.
> (1 Corinthians 10:13)

From what are we saved? In Jesus, our gateway to God, we are assured that one day we shall live free from the presence of sin. When we go to heaven there will be no sin. Speaking of heaven, God's word tells us, "Nothing unclean will enter it, nor anyone who practices abomination or falsehood" (Revelation 21:27). John writes,

> Beloved, we are God's children now; what we will be has not yet been revealed. What we do know is this: when he is revealed, we will be like him, for we will see him as he is. And all who have this hope in him purify themselves, just as he is pure.
> (1 John 3:2-3)

All these things are part of that marvelous proposition God makes to us in Jesus our gate.

Our Gate Is a Pasture

"I am the gate. Whoever enters by me will be saved, and will come in and go out and find pasture" (v. 9). Now allow your mind to go back to the great Shepherd Psalm, Psalm 23, where we read, "The Lord is my shepherd, I shall not want. He makes me lie down in green pastures; he leads me beside still waters; he restores my soul" (Psalm 23:1-3). Do you see it? There are two great promises in the opening words of this favorite psalm.

The first promise is that of a plentiful supply of all our needs: "I shall not want." Why shall I not want? Because the pastures where he leads are "green pastures." That is, the grass there is full and nutritious. Moreover, God's word also assures us, "My God will fully satisfy every need of yours according to his riches in glory in Christ Jesus" (Philippians 4:19). Abraham finds out how full that promise is long before Paul writes those words. On Mount Moriah, he sees God provide the necessary ram for sacrifice and we read, "So Abraham called that place 'The Lord will provide'; as it is said to this day, 'On the mount of the Lord it shall be provided' " (Genesis 22:14). In Jesus we no longer are searching for our needs because our needs are promised by our heavenly Father.

On the other hand, the false shepherd, says Jesus, "is a thief and a bandit" (v. 1). That is, someone who is out for what he can get for himself. He lives to get for himself. "The thief comes only to steal and kill and destroy," says Jesus. "I came that they may have life, and have it abundantly" (v. 10). The true shepherd is always focused on taking care of his sheep. He lives to give and that is why the sheep learn to trust him. Our true shepherd gave up his life for us and became our gate to the eternal pasture.

The second promise is that the sheep will find freedom in the pasture. No longer are the sheep hemmed in by their pen. Amazingly, there are people — even church people — whose image of coming to Jesus could be likened to spiritual incarceration. They sense that being a disciple of Jesus is akin to being locked up, insulated from reality as everyone else knows it, and from many experiences that would be fun and exciting. That kind of thinking is a myth with no basis in fact. Here Jesus depicts his sheep as enjoying true freedom. "Whoever enters by me will be saved, and will come in and out and find pasture" (v. 9). What is pasture but the lushest of living? How do the sheep find the lushest of pasture? By following the true shepherd who is always ahead of them preparing the way. Sheep who have no shepherd, on the other hand, are left to struggle through by their own devices. Wouldn't you rather be a sheep of the flock of a shepherd who gave up his own life for you that you "may have life, and have it abundantly"?

All this we find in Jesus. Have you found him looking for you? Where do you find yourself in relation to this wonderful passage? If you are still meandering around without a shepherd, if you are not saved, then I invite you right now to pause and acknowledge that you are a lost sheep and invite the great shepherd, Jesus, to come into your heart and take control of your life for today and every day until you go into that wonderful pasture he has prepared for you forevermore in his heaven.

Easter 5
John 14:1-14

The Power of the
Trust Factor

"Do not let your hearts be troubled. Believe in God, believe also
in me. In my Father's house there are many dwelling places. If
it were not so, would I have told you that I go to prepare a place
for you? And if I go and prepare a place for you, I will come
again and will take you to myself, so that where I am, there
you may be also. And you know the way to the place where I
am going." Thomas said to him, "Lord, we do not know where
you are going. How can we know the way?" Jesus said to him,
"I am the way, and the truth, and the life. No one comes to
the Father except through me. If you know me, you will know
my Father also. From now on you do know him and have seen
him." Philip said to him, "Lord, show us the Father, and we will
be satisfied." Jesus said to him, "Have I been with you all this
time, Philip, and you still do not know me? Whoever has seen
me has seen the Father. How can you say, 'Show us the Father'?
Do you not believe that I am in the Father and the Father is in
me? The words that I say to you I do not speak on my own; but
the Father who dwells in me does his works. Believe me that I
am in the Father and the Father is in me; but if you do not, then
believe me because of the works themselves. Very truly, I tell
you, the one who believes in me will also do the works that I
do and, in fact, will do greater works than these, because I am
going to the Father. I will do whatever you ask in my name, so
that the Father may be glorified in the Son. If in my name you
ask me for anything, I will do it."

How can we trust God when life seems to turn on us?
You know what I mean, I am sure. You are going through
life with ease and smoothness then all of a sudden things
begin to unravel. You put your head down and try harder but
it does not work. As one old saying puts it, "The harder I try

145

the behinder I get!" No one in all human history personifies those words better than Job. Scripture speaks glowingly of this good man, describing him as "blameless and upright." It says that Job "feared God." If the prosperity gospel were true, there is no one who would be more prosperous than Job. Don't take my word on Job. Listen to what scripture has to say about him: "There was once a man in the land of Uz whose name was Job. That man was blameless and upright, one who feared God and turned away from evil" (Job 1:1). It goes on to describe Job's beautiful family and holdings: "There were born to him seven sons and three daughters. He had seven thousand sheep, three thousand camels, five hundred yoke of oxen, five hundred donkeys, and very many servants; so that this man was the greatest of all the people of the east" (Job 1:2-3). I can imagine that if Job had an estate it would have to be something like *Downton Abbey*. Yet, as we study Job's story further, he loses his health, family, and wealth in a very short time. Job knows what it is to feel as though life were turning against him. He is hurt. His wife also is hurt and angry with God. His friends, who come to comfort him, only add salt to his wounds because they just do not understand what is going on behind Job's circumstances.

Despite all this, while Job is down he determines not to measure his life in terms of holdings or even friendships. His response is that of a man of amazing faith. On one occasion, Job says, "Though he slay me, I will hope in him" (Job 13:15 ESV). On another, he says, "He knows the way that I take; when he has tested me, I shall come out like gold" (Job 23:10). How can anybody say such things in response to such devastating loss? The answer is only by faith, a faith that holds onto God despite all else. That kind of faith does not come naturally to any of us. Pastors spend part of their lives on the edge of other people's tragedies and disappointments. There are times when we wonder how people can carry on after deep tragedy. Job is like that. His wife and his friends cannot relate to Job's response to the tragedies and pain he faces. He lives with a confidence that everything would come out all right in the end because his trust is not in what he has or even in those he has around him. Job's trust is in God alone. So near the close of his book we find him saying to God, "I know that you can do all things, and that no purpose of yours can be thwarted. 'Who is this that hides counsel without knowledge?' Therefore I have uttered what I did not understand, things too wonderful for me, which I did not know. 'Hear, and I will speak; I will question you, and you declare to me.' I had heard of you by the hearing of the ear, but now my eye sees you" (Job 42:1-5).

Today's scripture stands as an immoveable rock of trust when we come to moments like those Job experienced. Whether your heart is troubled just now, there is reason to believe it will be for as Job quickly realized, "man is born to trouble as the sparks fly upward" (cf., Job 5:7 ESV). John puts this certainty in these words: "In the world you face persecution" (John 16:33). The plain truth is that we all should expect to face hard times.

To understand what is happening as John 14 opens, we need to go back for a moment to John 13. This is one of the great pivotal moments in the life that Jesus and his disciples shared together. Jesus and his disciples have just eaten the Passover meal together for the last time. He takes a towel and washes the disciples' feet. He has just restated something he has already told them in a variety of ways before. Now, however, his words have a ring of finality to them. Clearly the time of his departure is nearer than ever before. In fact, it sounds imminent. He tells them that he will be betrayed and that his betrayer is one among them. Equally shocking is the fact that he says the disciple the others must have surely regarded as the strongest among them will deny him when he really needs a friend! Jesus' words stun them.

The words shatter the disciples' collective confidence. All, except perhaps the betrayer, Judas Iscariot, feel devastated.

Now comes chapter 14 to remind us that when the hard times come we are to accept them as part of life and continue to live with a deep inner peace. "Do not let your hearts be troubled. Believe in God, believe also in me" (v. 1). "Do not let" is a call for how we are to be personally engaged in facing tough times. We are not to sit by idly while our lives are under attack. We have God-given resources for every time of trouble. "Do not worry, saying, 'What will we eat?' or 'What will we drink?' or 'What will we wear?'... your heavenly Father knows that you need all these things. But strive first for the kingdom of God and his righteousness, and all these things will be given to you as well" (Matthew 6:31-33). "Cast all your anxiety on him, because he cares for you" (1 Peter 5:7). "Come to me, all you that are weary and are carrying heavy burdens, and I will give you rest" (Matthew 11:28). All these things Jesus has already taught the disciples as they walked together. So when he says, "Do not let your hearts be troubled. Believe in God, believe also in me," it is really a quick refresher course. The best way to handle life's tough times is to run to Jesus and be safe! Trust God! Trust Jesus!

Jesus tells his disciples that there is much more to life than this life: "In my Father's house there are many dwelling places. (The Greek word here, *monai*, is translated in the Latin Vulgate as *mansions*, which seems to capture the word 'mansions' used in other translations.) If it were not so, would I have told you that I go to prepare a place for you? And if I go and prepare a place for you, I will come again and will take you to myself, so that where I am, there you may be also" (vv. 2-3). While the trials and troubles we face are part of this life, reality is that we are not home yet and the difficulties of this life cannot follow us where we are headed. This prepared mansion is ours and it is already prepared by

Jesus who promises to come again and take us to where he is.

The presence of Jesus! It is all joy and pleasure. How can we know? Because God uses David the psalmist to say clearly, "You show me the path of life. In your presence there is fullness of joy; in your right hand are pleasures forevermore" (Psalm 16:11).

Jesus then announces to the disciples, "And you know the way to the place where I am going" (v. 4). The Lord could say this because he has been speaking about the faith that leads to eternal life with God. This has been the major theme of his teaching and preaching all through his ministry. For example, "Just as Moses lifted up the serpent in the wilderness, so must the Son of Man be lifted up, that whoever believes in him may have eternal life" (John 3:14-15).

Still the disciples do not fully understand what he is saying, and without a clear understanding of where Jesus is going, how could they know "the way." Thomas, seeming to speak for the rest of them, raises his voice in a question: "Lord, we do not know where you are going. How can we know the way?" (v. 5). It is a request for a definite word from Jesus about their eternal destination and how they would get there.

Now, like a GPS that hones in on our whereabouts from three coordinates, Jesus makes the answer more precise: "Jesus said to him, 'I am the way, and the truth, and the life. No one comes to the Father except through me' " (v. 6). Let's look at this verse of verses and see three things it said to them and says to us. The three concepts are simple to remember if we assign them each a word.

Salvation!
"Jesus said to him, 'I am the way' " (v. 6).

The first time the term Christian (which is derived from the term "Christ Ones") was used to define the followers of

Jesus Christ was in Antioch, Syria (Acts 11:26). Until that time, the more general name for Christ's followers was simply "people of the way." Saul of Tarsus, for example, planned to go to Damascus to search out "any who belonged to the Way, men or women" (Acts 9:2). The name was born out of the lifestyle of the early Christians. Their way of living — not their words — designated them as disciples.

A pastor friend took a trip to Ireland with his wife. At the airport in Dublin they rented a car and set out to drive to their first night's accommodations. They had not been driving long when they realized they were lost. Stopping in a village square, they asked a local: "How do we get to Ballymacswindle?" The man said, "Let me take you there." With a certain amount of trepidation, they opened the car door and allowed a stranger to sit beside them. At first the two of them were thinking about what they had done. Silently, the man and his wife each thought, "Who is this fellow? Why is he so friendly? Is this a set up?" It was not. They later reported that it was a wonderful trip. As he gave them directions, their new passenger regaled them with stories about the history and personalities in every village they encountered. When someone offers to take us to the place where we want to go, that offer goes far beyond just telling us the way. That person, in fact, becomes our companion for the journey. That is what Jesus says to his disciples and to us in these words, "I will take you to the Father."

In our postmodern world, some people — even some church people — say that all roads lead to heaven. Jesus disagrees! "No one comes to the Father except through me," he says. What might have happened had my pastor friend not accepted the offer of the man he asked for directions? He very possibly would have gone farther in the wrong direction. Many people think that the way to heaven comes by doing good deeds, working hard, or trying their best. That is not what the Bible says. Nowhere do we read, "Do your best and heaven is yours." Nowhere does scripture say. "A good moral life is enough."

There is only one way to heaven and it is through Jesus. I know this teaching offends some people but these are not our rules. These are God's standards. People who believe Jesus is the only way are sometimes considered narrow-minded. But do you know why this truth bugs some people? It is because Satan hates truth. The Bible calls him, "the father of lies" (John 8:44).

Sincerity!

"Jesus said to him, 'I am the way, and the truth' " (v. 6).

When Jesus calls himself "the truth," he means that he is the truth about God for all generations and that all knowledge begins and ends in him. That reality has not changed in 2,000 years. It will never change because truth as Jesus means it is objective truth. It is not truth that depends on public opinion polls. It is the same in darkness and light. It is true on every continent and on every planet. Objective truth is that which, when you stop believing it, does not go away. When Jesus becomes our "truth," we step up to a level of learning that will be constant for all eternity. No one can get any more certainty than that!

As God's truth, Jesus tells us three things about God: First, he tells us that people can know God personally and intimately through his Son. Second, he tells us that God cares more about us than about himself. If you ever doubt that let me remind you of that Friday afternoon at calvary when God gave up his own Son for us. Third, Jesus does not offer us yet one more religion to add to the world's list of religions. Instead, he offers us a relationship with himself.

In this one statement, Jesus Christ puts his credibility on the line as no one else in all history for either he is who he says he is or he has misled more people than all of history's cruelest tricksters combined. If Jesus is not "the truth," every

151

great movement begun in his name is a house built on sinking sand, everyone who ever laid claim to being a disciple is a fool, and every great hymn of tribute that Christians sing to Jesus is of no more spiritual significance than, "You Ain't Nuthin' But a Hound Dog!" Without his way there is no going; without his truth, there is no knowing.

Satisfaction!

"Jesus said to him, 'I am the way, and the truth, and the life' " (v. 6).

When Jesus calls himself "the life," his definition of life is so large that the Greek language has a special word for it. The common Greek word for life, *bios*, gives us our English words biology, biological, and so on. Biological life can be measured in terms of its beginning and ending. For Christ "life," the Greek word is *zoeh*, means life without limits; life that is immeasurable in terms of its length and depth. We have no idea how big our lives will be until we trust him for new life.

Where is your life leading you? If you died today, where will you spend this evening? Where will you go when you die? Jesus says, "Because I live, you also will live" (John 14:19). But, where will we live forever? That is the most important question that will ever confront us.

There are just two ways to get to heaven. The first way is the Plan A way. The A stands for accomplishment. To get to heaven under this plan all you have to do is live perfectly from the moment you are born until the moment you die. That is it: Just be perfect. Never make a mistake. Never think an evil thought. Never say an evil word. Never do anything that is not completely perfect. If you can do that, you can qualify for heaven under Plan A.

My guess is that none of us qualify for Plan A. So let me tell you about the only other way to get to heaven. It is called Plan B. The B stands for Believe in Jesus. Because he knew that none of us would qualify under Plan A, God came up with Plan B. Under this plan we begin by admitting to God that we cannot qualify for Plan A. We need to believe Jesus Christ when he says, "I am the way, the truth and the life." He was the only person who ever qualified for Plan A and by trusting in his perfection and establishing a relationship with him, we get in on his goodness.

Without Jesus' way, there is no going. Without his truth, there is no knowing. Without his life, there is no growing. These are life's three firm foundations. Now go out into the world to build your life with him and you will live the life abundant.

Our only hope is to trust him! That is the power of the trust factor!

This Spirit Is Not Spooky

If you love me, you will keep my commandments. And I will ask the Father, and he will give you another Advocate, to be with you forever. This is the Spirit of truth, whom the world cannot receive, because it neither sees him nor knows him. You know him, because he abides with you, and he will be in you. I will not leave you orphaned; I am coming to you. In a little while the world will no longer see me, but you will see me; because I live, you also will live. On that day you will know that I am in my Father, and you in me, and I in you. They who have my commandments and keep them are those who love me; and those who love me will be loved by my Father, and I will love them and reveal myself to them.

These words were spoken just hours before the greatest act of love in world history, the death on a cross of God's incarnate Son, the Lord Jesus Christ. He died in our place so that everyone who believes on him (Mark you, not *in*, but *on* him — and there is a difference. To believe *in* something can be seen as nothing more than an exercise of intellectual assent for we remember that we are told, "Even the demons believe — and shudder" [James 2:19]. To believe "on" him means to lay our whole lives on him and trust him completely. It means to follow his commands with complete obedience.) will be forgiven all their sins and accepted as righteous by God and admitted into the never-ending joy of eternal life. What Jesus is saying here assumes that. He is, as he said in John 10:15, about to lay down his life for his sheep. The sheep who immediately hear these words — the eleven closest friends of Jesus — are confused, uncertain, and fearful at hearing them. So Jesus gives them a promise, "I will ask the Father, and he will give you another Advocate, to be with you forever" (v. 16). His message to them, and to us, is one of everlasting assurance. Let us consider this other advocate, the Holy Spirit, who comes to us from Jesus and the Father to be with us forever, and never leave us, no matter where we are or what is happening to us.

> I will ask the Father, and he will give you another Advocate, to be with you forever. This is the Spirit of truth, whom the world cannot receive, because it neither sees him nor knows him. You know him, because he abides with you, and he will be in you. (vv. 16-17)

How would you like to know you had a friend whose very name is a promise to be the best friend you could ever hope for? Who says that no matter what your past, it can be forgiven, who will pick you up when you are down, and meet you wherever you are and look out for you? You do have someone like that. His power energizes everything good in the church, and in Christians, since Jesus' ascension. His name is Holy Spirit.

Stephen Carter, a Yale law professor, in his book *The Culture of Disbelief,* traces the decline of Christian influence in America and concludes that our future is abysmally ominous. That will surprise no thinking Christian. Long ago Solomon prophesied, "Where there is no prophecy, the people cast off restraint" (Proverbs 29:18). The result of ungodliness is always unrestraint, which, in turn, results in spiritual death. A nation that locks God out of its public life is guaranteed to die. Nor should we expect God's blessing when his word has no bearing on our private — or church — life. How can one expect blessing from a power we neither know nor honor? The Bible says we know God only through Jesus Christ, who died on the cross to take away our sins and rose again. Jesus says, "No one comes to the Father except through me" (John 14:6). If you want to know God, get to know Jesus. How do we know we know Jesus? Through the Holy Spirit, for we read,

> For all who are led by the Spirit of God are children of God. For you did not receive a spirit of slavery to fall back into fear, but you have received a spirit of adoption. When we cry, 'Abba! Father!' it is that very Spirit bearing witness with our spirit that we are children of God.
> (Romans 8:14-16)

"This is the Spirit of truth, whom the world cannot receive, because it neither sees him nor knows him. You know him, because he abides with you, and he will be in you" (v. 17). The late atheist, Madeline O'Hare, often referred disrespectfully to the Holy Spirit as "the spook." Webster defines spook as a frightening object. In Madeline O'Hare's world, the Holy Spirit was like a scary Halloween ghost.

How does your mind visualize the Holy Spirit? As something or someone mysterious? As a weird agent of fear, despair, and doubt? Or, is your image of the Holy Spirit different from these images? When we look at the Bible we see a picture of the Holy Spirit revealed in several different images.

The Spirit Portrayed!

First, we see him as being likened to fire when John the Baptist says: "I baptize you with water; but one who is more powerful than I is coming; I am not worthy to untie the thong of his sandals. He will baptize you with the Holy Spirit and fire" (Luke 3:16). The presence of only one article before "Holy Spirit" and "fire" in the Greek text in this passage suggests that John means the description to speak of only one baptism. The Holy Spirit comes like fire, the symbol of purification that sanctifies us and makes us fit for heaven.

157

On Pentecost Day, we see the Holy Spirit likened to wind:

> Suddenly from heaven there came a sound like the rush of a violent wind, and it filled the entire house where they were sitting... All of them were filled with the Holy Spirit and began to speak in other languages, as the Spirit gave them ability.
> (Acts 2:2, 4)

Jesus uses the same image when he speaks with Nicodemus and says, "The wind blows where it chooses, and you hear the sound of it, but you do not know where it comes from or where it goes. So it is with everyone who is born of the Spirit" (John 3:8). That is to say, the Spirit is unpredictable and uncontrollable. Think of those coastal hurricane winds, such as Hurricane Katrina from the Gulf of Mexico and Hurricane Sandy from the Atlantic. Their winds are powerful and can tear away what is weak and unsafe. So also the Holy Spirit strips away the false shelters in which we try to hide from God. Then again, walk across San Francisco's Golden Gate Bridge, catch the breeze there, and experience how wind also refreshes! The Spirit of God blows away our spiritual cobwebs and brings new life wherever he moves.

We also see God's Holy Spirit likened to water. Jesus says,

> Let anyone who is thirsty come to me, and let the one who believes in me drink. As the scripture has said, "Out of the believer's heart shall flow rivers of living water." Now he said this about the Spirit.
> (John 7:37-39)

Only Jesus in the power of the Holy Spirit can satisfy our craving for real life. Let me tell you how this happens: Your life feels drab and you reason, "There has to be more." You are correct! The Holy Spirit brings refreshment to our dreariness and we come alive again.

We find allusions to the dove also when scripture speaks about the Spirit: "John testified, 'I saw the Spirit descending from heaven like a dove' " (John 1:32). Since the time of Noah, the dove is a symbol of peace. Paul, remembering this, writes: "Since we are justified by faith, we have peace with God through our Lord Jesus Christ... because God's love has been poured into our hearts through the Holy Spirit that has been given to us" (Romans 5:1, 5). When the Holy Spirit comes upon our lives, we have peace beyond our understanding.

These beautiful, powerful, and eloquent signs express the Holy Spirit's work but they miss the essence and vitality of the Bible's description of the Holy Spirit's personality.

The Spirit's Personality!

John 14 uses a series of personal pronouns to teach us that the Holy Spirit is true personality and not an "it" as he is often spoken about. Sometimes we have difficulty comprehending the personality of the Holy Spirit. We have this sense that since the Holy Spirit emanates from the Father and the Son, he must therefore be something of a lesser God, or perhaps not even a God at all but an instrument of God. We can imagine the Father as a personality because we see him hanging the universe with the planets and stars, each in its own place. We know that he calls each of them by name. We can believe in his personality because we see his acts in nature. Similarly, we can more readily understand Jesus, the Son, as personality because we remember him as a baby in a Bethlehem manger. We see him walking on earth and talking to other people. We follow his persecution in Pilate's hall and being nailed to the cross for our sins. We anticipate him coming again to judge the living and the dead and wearing the crown of heaven for all eternity. It does not stretch our imagination to see Jesus as a person.

But the Holy Spirit seems different somehow; his ways are more mysterious and secret with the result that many Christians do not think of him as having personality. Reality is that the Holy Spirit is as much personality as either the Father or the Son. The deity of the Holy Spirit is clearly recognized in scripture. Look at these facts: Christ is born; the Spirit is his forerunner. Christ is baptized; the Spirit bears witness to who he is. Christ is tempted; the Spirit leads him up to the wilderness. Christ ascends; the Spirit takes his place. Or think of the Holy Spirit as being present when we baptize someone in the church. The standard baptismal formula, "I baptize you in the name of the Father, and of the Son, and of the Holy Spirit." We did not say the "names," but the "name." It is one name and not a plurality of names. The Father, Son, and Holy Spirit are one person.

Perhaps the foremost indicator of the Spirit's personality comes from the apostle Paul when he writes about the Spirit's speculation: "God, who searches the heart, knows what is the mind of the Spirit, because the Spirit intercedes for the saints according to the will of God" (Romans 8:27). On another occasion, Paul writes of the Spirit's awareness: "No one comprehends what is truly God's except the Spirit of God" (1 Corinthians 2:11). An impersonal being, an "it," cannot possess the ability to understand a living being. Because the Spirit has personality, he can relate to the living God. Because he is part of the godhead, he can understand God.

We also read that the Holy Spirit communicates. Peter says to the other disciples, "Friends, the scripture had to be fulfilled, which the Holy Spirit through David foretold concerning Judas" (Acts 1:16). What a fascinating statement about the Holy Spirit speaking and about scripture's inspiration and authority! Later in the same book, we read: "While they were worshiping the Lord and fasting, the Holy Spirit said, 'Set apart for me Barnabas and Saul for the work to which I have called them' " (Acts 13:2). He speaks. I believe he speaks today. Otherwise, how can we explain that someone is "called" to do this or "led" to do that? Sometimes we hear testimonies of people whose lives were turned in a completely different direction from what they had been planning. Who is it that calls or leads us in new ways but the Holy Spirit?

Another indicator of the personality of the Holy Spirit is that he has the capacity to feel emotion. Paul writes of "the love of the Spirit" (Romans 15:30). Paul also notes that he "cries" in Galatians 4:6 and that he is grieved in Ephesians 4:30. In 2 Corinthians 13:13, Paul writes of the Spirit communing with Christians. In Acts 5:3, Paul challenges Ananias with these words "Peter asked, 'Why has Satan filled your heart to lie to the Holy Spirit?' " One cannot lie to that which is inanimate, but one can lie to a person. The Holy Spirit is a person. He is the godhead's third person!

The Spirit — Our Proponent!

The Holy Spirit came on Old Testament believers temporarily to give them strength. Normally, however, he did not remain with them. The guilt-ridden David pleads with God, "Do not cast me away from your presence, and do not take your Holy Spirit from me" (Psalm 51:11). What Jesus presents here is new, different, and exciting. Now the Spirit comes to stay with us for the rest of our lives. Listen for the word "forever"! Jesus said, "I will ask the Father, and he will give you another Advocate, to be with you forever" (v. 16).

The Greek word for Advocate is *parakletos*, which is a joining together of two Greek words. The first part of this word is *para*, which denotes the idea of supporting or helping. The second part is from the Greek word *kaleoh*, from which we derive our English verb "to call." So a reasonable translation would be "someone who is called to support or help." Let me suggest another translation: "One helper beside the called." That is, the Holy Spirit stands tall with those who come when Christ calls. Some of us know the Holy Spirit's comfort. We have walked through some of life's dark valleys. We have come to the end of our rope and have found, somehow, new strength to carry on against all odds. Perhaps you have struggled against doubt and despair, and you have felt unseen arms support you when you know that once upon a time you would have fainted.

The Karre language of equatorial Africa proved to be especially difficult for the translators of the Karre New Testament, especially when it came to the word *parakletos*. How could they describe the role of the Holy Spirit? One day a couple of translators came across a group of porters going off into the bush carrying bundles on their heads. They noticed that in the line of porters there was one who did not carry anything on his head, and they assumed he must be the boss who was there to make sure the others did their work. However, they learned that he was not the boss. The man with no bundle had a particular job. He was there should someone carrying a bundle become overloaded and be unable to carry on. The man with no bundle would step in and pick up that weak man's load and help him carry it. This porter was known in the Karre language as "the one who shares the load beside us." Suddenly, those translators had their word for *parakletos*. That is what the Holy Spirit does for us.

It must also be said that the Holy Spirit can seem like a very discomforting Advocate. We remember that he wrestled Jacob and would not let go. In church history, we find him during a time when it seems that the days of the gospel are on the wane. He comes with a glorious fresh breeze of revival power and everything is renewed and faith becomes exciting again as the church comes alive once more. He convicts us of, and delivers us from, sin. He changes lives.

"The Spirit intercedes for the saints according to the will of God" (Romans 8:27). Our spiritual focus is transformed from self-centeredness into world-centered ministry. We go from maintenance to ministry, from issues to evangelism, from what used to be to what can be. In the Spirit's power, passion for Jesus is paramount. May it please God to do it with us and with our church! Please pray to that end.

We read, "another Advocate." The Greek word means "another one like the first one." It stands in opposition to another Greek word that means "another that is a different from the one before." Jesus is telling them, and through them, us, that he and the Holy Spirit are one in design and ministry. That is, they are perfect partners. Jesus our first Advocate was gloriously and wonderfully committed to us all the way to the cross. Now Jesus is saying that we are to be ready to meet our other Advocate, God's Holy Spirit. Like Jesus, he is our proponent who wants what is best for us. But his best will not come unless we are totally committed to what he is about in our world.

This is the Holy Spirit, our Advocate, and he is present wherever two or more are gathered in Jesus' name. Today, the Holy Spirit is here looking out for you, for each of us. "Therefore, brothers and sisters, be all the more eager to confirm your call and election, for if you do this, you will never stumble" (2 Peter 1:10). I invite you to respond by entering into a personal walk with him and commit your life firmly to Christ and his church.

When you do that, you will find the Holy Spirit, and he will find you!

Ascension of Our Lord
Luke 24:44-53

The Time Is Now!

Then he said to them, "These are my words that I spoke to you while I was still with you — that everything written about me in the Law of Moses, the prophets, and the psalms must be fulfilled." Then he opened their minds to understand the scriptures, and he said to them, "Thus it is written, that the Messiah is to suffer and to rise from the dead on the third day, and that repentance and forgiveness of sins is to be proclaimed in his name to all nations, beginning from Jerusalem. You are witnesses of these things. And see, I am sending upon you what my Father promised; so stay here in the city until you have been clothed with power from on high." Then he led them out as far as Bethany, and, lifting up his hands, he blessed them. While he was blessing them, he withdrew from them and was carried up into heaven. And they worshiped him, and returned to Jerusalem with great joy; and they were continually in the temple blessing God.

Unlike John or Peter, the gospel writer Luke was a cool-headed intellect. Luke was a physician. As a physician, he was trained to keep his emotional distance from the events he saw. Nobody wants a physician who lets emotion run ahead of intellect. We want our medical doctors to be able to confront the most remarkable experiences and stay calm; to analyze, decide the best course of action, and prescribe whatever it takes to get the patient well again. Above all else, "Keep calm and carry on." That is, do not let the moment possess you. Yet there was one moment in the life of Jesus that so impressed Luke that he could not stay calm. He had to tell it. In fact, it so impressed the physician-follower that he wrote about it on two different occasions. Luke understood that this was the moment when history and modernity came together; when heaven met earth as never before for Jesus and his first disciples. That moment in time was the ascension of Jesus into heaven. Luke writes about it here at the close of his gospel. Next, he records it again as he begins the book of Acts.

As Luke closes out his record about the life of Jesus, he writes: "Then he led them out as far as Bethany, and, lifting up his hands, he blessed them. While he was blessing them, he withdrew from them and was carried up into heaven" (vv. 50-51).

In Acts 1, the same Luke records that moment in these words:

"In the first book, Theophilus, I wrote about all that Jesus did and taught from the beginning until the day when he was taken up to heaven, after giving instructions through the Holy Spirit to the apostles whom he had chosen. After his suffering he presented himself alive to them by many convincing proofs, appearing to them during forty days and speaking about the kingdom of God. While staying with them, he ordered them not to leave Jerusalem, but to wait there for the promise of the Father. 'This,' he said, 'is what you have heard from me; for John baptized with water, but you will be baptized with the Holy Spirit not many days from now.' So when they had come together, they asked him, 'Lord, is this the time when you will restore the kingdom to Israel?' He replied, 'It is not for you to know the times or periods that the Father has set by his own authority. But you will receive power when the Holy Spirit has come upon you; and you will be my witnesses in Jerusalem, in all Judea and Samaria, and to the ends of the earth.' When he had said this, as they were watching, he was lifted up, and a cloud took him out of their sight. While he was going and they were gazing up toward heaven, suddenly two men in white robes stood by them. They said, 'Men of Galilee, why do you stand looking up toward heaven? This Jesus, who has been taken up from you into heaven, will come in the same way as you saw him go into heaven.' Then they returned to Jerusalem from the mount

called Olivet, which is near Jerusalem, a sabbath day's journey away."
(Acts 1:1-12)

Did you catch it? Did you spot what looks at first glance like a Bible discrepancy? Luke's gospel says the ascension takes place in Bethany, but in Acts 1:12 the same author records that Mount Olivet was the place. Is it really a discrepancy? No. In fact, anyone who has visited the Holy Land soon discovers that if someone is on the Mount of Olives, he can be said to be at Bethany. The two locations are so close in proximity that the two names are used interchangeably, even today.

We celebrate Ascension Sunday one day each year on the church calendar. However, we affirm Christ's ascension every time we say the Apostles' Creed, "He (Jesus) ascended into heaven and sits at the right hand of God the Father almighty."

Now, here we are, two millennia later. We are well ordered and well run. For 2,000 years the church has been affirming the ascension. We have everything we need to really make a positive and eternal difference in our communities and our world, except one thing: Where is the "power from on high"? Why have we not, in our generation, fulfilled this command to go out in Christ's power? Is it because so many of us have not taken this promise as authentic? Would things be different if we ordered our lives by it? Given this, my question is how much do we think about what the ascension really means and how much does it impact our daily lives? In Luke's record of the final discourse between Jesus and his disciples, Jesus recollects some highlight events of his life on earth before commissioning them to carry on his work. He recalls his suffering and resurrection. He relates it all to the Old Testament: " 'These are my words that I spoke to you while I was still with you — that everything written about me in the Law of Moses, the prophets, and the psalms must be fulfilled.' Then he opened their minds to understand the scriptures" (vv. 44-45).

History and Modernity Meet in Christ's Ascension

Think once more about what we say in the Apostles' Creed: "He ascended into heaven and sits at the right hand of God the Father almighty." Now listen once more and allow the transitional tense of verb sink in this time: "He ascended (past tense) into heaven and sits (present tense) at the right hand of God the Father almighty."

Through this one sentence, we know we are different from our non-Christian friends. We have an answer they do not have. "Where is your Jesus when life makes no sense?" the skeptic asks. Our answer is that he is at the right hand of God where, "He is able for all time to save those who approach God through him, since he always lives to make intercession for them" (Hebrews 7:25).

History and modernity come together in the ascension of God's Son, Jesus, as in no other world religious system or philosophy. We can say, "He died for me and he lives for me!" What a mighty master!

To whom can anyone compare our Jesus? "I serve a risen Savior,"[1] the old hymn says. We sing it and say, "He lives, He lives, salvation to impart! You ask me how I know He lives: He lives within my heart." That is true but it is not the best part of its truthfulness. The best part of its truthfulness is that he was witnessed ascending on high and "when he ascended on high he made captivity itself a captive; he gave gifts to his people." (When it says, "He ascended," what does it mean but that he had also descended into the lower parts of the earth? He who descended is the same one who ascended far above all the heavens, so that he might fill all things.) (Ephesians 4:8-10).

History and modernity meet in God's Son Jesus. We

know where Jesus is and what he is doing there. In Romans 12 and 1 Corinthians 12 Paul speaks of gifts given to people. In Ephesians 4, Paul speaks of people given to the church as gifts by the ascended *Christus victor*. In his death and resurrection, Jesus overcomes the hostile powers that hold people in subjection; those powers of the devil, sin, the law, and death are conquered in the Lord's resurrection. Just as an Old Testament military victor has the right to give gifts to those identified with him, so Jesus Christ, who conquered sin on the cross, has the right to give those who follow him to the church along with the gifts he has placed in them. Following his resurrection and after forty days with his disciples, Jesus is taken up to heaven where he sits with the Father, pleading our cause. He bridges the gap between the eternal God and people in our generation.

Philosophy and Practicality Meet in Jesus' Ascension

Repentance and forgiveness of sins is to be proclaimed in his name to all nations, beginning from Jerusalem. You are witnesses of these things. And see, I am sending upon you what my Father promised; so stay here in the city until you have been clothed with power from on high.
(vv. 47-49)

Now we come to something else that sets Christians and Christianity apart from every other philosophy or religion: that is, the practicality of the gospel of Jesus. This gospel works and it puts us to work. Christianity is not a spectator sport. Think again about all the statements of the Apostles' Creed that precede the declaration of Christ's ascension. They fall under the heading of forensic theology. That is, they are foundation stones for our Christian belief system.

I believe in God the Father, Almighty,
Creator of heaven and earth.

169

I believe in Jesus Christ, God's only Son, our Lord,
Who was conceived by the Holy Spirit,
born of the Virgin Mary,
Suffered under Pontius Pilate,
was crucified, dead, and was buried,
he descended to the dead.
On the third day he rose again;
he ascended into heaven,
he is seated at the right hand of the Father.

Our scripture reading about the Lord's ascension makes it clear that we are not to rest on Christ's laurels, uncaring and uninvolved in the world we are called to live in for now. When Jesus ascended, all the work of the gospel was not done. There is a world to be won and there are people to be served and issues to be addressed. In short, Christianity is more than a religious philosophy. It brings to those who become disciples a practical responsibility.

At his ascension, Jesus hands the torch of his gospel to us. The late Dutch pastor John DeVries lets his imagination picture what might have happened when Jesus entered heaven at his ascension. The angels rejoiced. Their master's earthly mission was accomplished. They welcomed him home. They remembered how in the past one of them was always used to carry God's good news to earthlings. Like school children vying for their teacher's favor, they jostled among themselves for who might be given the privilege of telling the world God's new good news. Christ was born, lived, died on a Roman cross, and rose from the dead to provide salvation from sin. They waited anxiously for the answer to their question. Jesus pointed back to the little band of followers he had just left behind, "There they are. They will be my witnesses. They have experienced the thrill of redemption and they will tell my story to the world."

The gospel torch that was handed over to the church in Jerusalem has been carried down through generations and across continents until today, when we hold it and determine what future, if any, it has. The reality of the ascension of Jesus is this: We have work to do.

Our Lord has already indicated this in his parables of the talents, each is designed to help the people who first heard them know that his kingdom is not to come immediately. Many of the people who follow him expect the kingdom to be fulfilled when Jesus reaches Jerusalem. These parables should have dispelled those hopes but it seems they do not for: They asked him, "Lord, is this the time when you will restore the kingdom to Israel?" (Acts 1:6). The disciples fail to understand that each of those parables speaks of work to be done by the servants of the king. Even though the Son of Man came to seek out and to save the lost (Luke 19:10), the national deliverance of Israel must wait. In the parables, the nobleman represents Jesus. The far country he travels to stands for heaven, and the place he will return to is the earth. Jesus goes to heaven to receive the kingdom from his Father.

In the meantime, we have work to do. For 2,000 years now, the followers of Jesus Christ have been carrying out his work around the world, whether in a hospital to bring health and healing in Chonju, Korea; a school to educate Maasai children in East Africa; or a church to spread the gospel in the former Soviet Union. On every continent more work for human advancement has been done in the history of the world by the disciples of the ascended Christ than by all other groups — religious or otherwise, in the history of the world, including most of America's historic ivy league institutions. Now add to these individuals the number of helping organizations that have been established in Christ's name and you begin to get some sense of how philosophy and practicality meet in the ascended Jesus. The Christian faith is nothing if not practical.

In time, the disciples were "clothed with power from on

high" (v. 49). The Greek word for "power" is *dunamis*, the root of our English words dynamic, dynamo, and dynamite! Behind it is the idea that those who have this power can do anything with God's might behind them. This power is limitless. In ourselves we are weak and can do only limited things. Paul, whom we often think of as unlimited in power and potential, tells us, "I know that nothing good dwells within me, that is, in my flesh. I can will what is right, but I cannot do it" (Romans 7:18). But he also knows, "I can do all things through him who strengthens me" (Philippians 4:13). Both statements come from the same man and both are true. The question is which one will we allow to guide us? I submit to you that what we accomplish for the Lord comes about to a large degree because of which of these two statements we decide to follow. Eleven ordinary men clothed with God's dynamic power literally changed their world. They were not super men. Their ways were not otherworldly. They were practical. What they did worked because the gospel of the ascended Jesus Christ is nothing if not practical.

It can happen again. It can happen now. It can happen through us. A.W. Tozer said, "Anything God has ever done, he can do now! Anything God has ever done anywhere else he can do here! Anything God has ever done for anyone else, he can do for you!" Do you believe that? Of course you do because philosophy (what we believe) and practicality (what we do) meet in Jesus Christ's ascension.

Time and Eternity Meet in Christ's Ascension

Lifting up his hands, he blessed them. While he was blessing them, he withdrew from them and was carried up into heaven. And they worshiped him, and returned to Jerusalem with great joy; and they were continually in the temple blessing God. (vv. 50-53)

In my Father's house there are many dwelling places. If it were not so, would I have told you that I go to prepare a place for you? And if I go and prepare a place for you, I will come again and will take you to myself, so that where I am, there you may be also... "I am the way, and the truth, and the life. No one comes to the Father except through me." (John 14:2-3, 6)

Time and eternity meet in Christ's ascension. So far, we have considered the practical application of the gospel of the ascended Jesus on every continent, but his work is higher and better even than that. There is a further practical implication in Jesus' ascension. His physical part in earthly ministry accomplished, he yet had a heavenly mission to fulfill. He left to prepare our place in the Father's house.

Heaven is a promised, prepared, perfect, paid-for place for prepared people. The Lord of heaven himself prepares our place there. We get there as a gift simply by taking him at his word. In his ascension, our ascension is guaranteed. We shall reign with him in glory. Meanwhile, we are charged to bring the message of heaven to earth.

So "why do you stand looking up toward heaven? This Jesus, who has been taken up from you into heaven, will come in the same way as you saw him go into heaven" (Acts 1:11). That question asked by the ascension angels still has merit. The Bible says that when we least expect him, the ascended Christ is coming again. If he came today, what would you want him to find you doing for his church and his kingdom? Go and do it for Jesus' sake!

During World War I a talented young concert pianist was drafted and sent to the front line. His right arm was horribly mangled in a fierce battle. Medics recognized that unless they amputated that arm, the young musician would die. They amputated the ruined arm. Devastated, yet determined, the young man refused to allow the loss of his arm to destroy him. He was discharged and shipped home, a one-

173

armed piano player. He trekked from composer to composer asking for any piano compositions they might have written or know of for only the left hand. He found none. Finally, he visited Maurice Ravel, the brilliant French composer of *Bolero* and himself a veteran of that war. Ravel responded to the young musician's need by writing a new piano concerto, *The Ravel Concerto in D Major for Left Hand.* For years to come, audiences throughout Europe were stirred by the passion with which that young pianist rendered that piece. He could not play the two-handed pieces but he could play this one!

Jesus, our ascended Lord, is coming again. Whatever you imagine is your handicap, whatever you imagine is your limitation, there is kingdom work for you to do. In the name of Jesus, go out and play your piece with passion. Do all the good you can to all the people you can for Jesus who loved us all the way to calvary and loves us still. Don't stand around looking up, do something! You will soon discover that the place where you have been planted is the place where your deep gladness and this world's deep hunger come together.

There is a time when heaven and earth come together. That time is now!

---

1. "He Lives," Alfred H. Ackley, 1934.

Easter 7
John 17:1-11

The Biggest Prayer Ever Prayed Under Heaven!

After Jesus had spoken these words, he looked up to heaven and said, "Father, the hour has come; glorify your Son so that the Son may glorify you, since you have given him authority over all people, to give eternal life to all whom you have given him. And this is eternal life, that they may know you, the only true God, and Jesus Christ whom you have sent. I glorified you on earth by finishing the work that you gave me to do. So now, Father, glorify me in your own presence with the glory that I had in your presence before the world existed. I have made your name known to those whom you gave me from the world. They were yours, and you gave them to me, and they have kept your word. Now they know that everything you have given me is from you; for the words that you gave to me I have given to them, and they have received them and know in truth that I came from you; and they have believed that you sent me. I am asking on their behalf; I am not asking on behalf of the world, but on behalf of those whom you gave me, because they are yours. All mine are yours, and yours are mine; and I have been glorified in them. And now I am no longer in the world, but they are in the world, and I am coming to you. Holy Father, protect them in your name that you have given me, so that they may be one, as we are one."

Come with me to Christ's last night on earth and the greatest prayer ever prayed under heaven! It is also the longest prayer we have from Jesus. As we read the gospel of John, we see Jesus' grace demonstrated in saving sinners. We see his compassionate heart as he brings healing to sick people and food to the hungry. We meet his power revealed in raising the dead. There is no more heartening book in all scripture than this gospel. Every chapter is given for our benefit. In this book we find the love of God demonstrated and explained as nowhere else. Like a pinnacle, John 17 rises above the other high peaks in John's book. Here we are allowed to glimpse into Jesus' very soul. We never get any closer to someone than when we know about their prayer life. So it is not overstating anything to say that when we come to this chapter we are entering holy ground and we should come in a spirit of reverence and humility, expecting to be touched in a very deep way.

The *Westminster Shorter Catechism* Question 23 asks, then answers, a question: "What offices does Christ execute as our redeemer?" The answer is, "Christ, as our redeemer, executes the offices of a prophet, of a priest, and of a king, both in his estate of humiliation and exaltation." This passage from John's gospel brings us face-to-face with Jesus' priestly office. In the letter to the Hebrews we read,

> Brothers and sisters, holy partners in a heavenly calling, consider that Jesus, the apostle and high priest of our confession, was faithful to the one who appointed him.
> (Hebrews 3:1-2)

> We have this hope, a sure and steadfast anchor of the soul, a hope that enters the inner shrine behind the curtain, where Jesus, a forerunner on our behalf, has entered, having become a high priest forever according to the order of Melchizedek.
> (Hebrews 6:19-20)

Hebrew priesthood was no shallow office. The Bible names at least three necessary foundational parts for priesthood.

First, priesthood calls for inward cleansing. Not only is the priestly office of divine institution, the priest has a personal, divine obligation to live an exemplary life. "Every high priest chosen from among mortals is put in charge of things pertaining to God... one does not presume to take this honor, but takes it only when called by God" (Hebrews 5:1, 4). At the beginning of his earthly ministry, Jesus said: "The Spirit of the Lord is upon me, because he has anointed me to bring good news to the poor. He has sent me to proclaim release to the captives and recovery of sight to the blind, to let the oppressed go free" (Luke 4:18). The priest always begins his time of prayer with a personal confession of his own sins. He knows that the psalmist says: "If I had cherished iniquity in my heart, the Lord would not have listened" (Psalm 66:18).

Priesthood secondly demands upward communication. The office of priest is God's gracious provision for a people who need someone who can advocate for the people when he comes into God's presence and then take God's word to the people. The role of the priest is to speak for God. Scripture says of the priest: "Every high priest chosen from among mortals is put in charge of things pertaining to God" (Hebrews 5:1).

Third, the priesthood calls for intercession on behalf of the people. The priest takes God's word to the people. Conversely, the priest brings the people's sins before God. He does this so that the people might know forgiveness and reconciliation with their maker. This is where the priesthood calls for sacrifice, probably the best-known priestly function of all in scripture. "Every high priest chosen from among mortals is put in charge of things pertaining to God on their behalf, to offer gifts and sacrifices for sins" (Hebrews 5:1). Before that can happen, the priest "had to become like his brothers and sisters in every respect, so that he might be a merciful and faithful high priest in the service of God, to make a sacrifice of atonement for the sins of the people" (Hebrews 2:17). Priesthood is not otherworldly. There can be no effective advocacy on behalf of sinners until their guilt is acknowledged and atoned before God. It is the priest's job to do this as he represents the people before the almighty.

> Aaron lifted his hands toward the people and blessed them; and
> he came down after sacrificing the sin offering, the burnt offer-
> ing, and the offering of well-being. Moses and Aaron entered
> the tent of meeting, and then came out and blessed the people;
> and the glory of the Lord appeared to all the people.
> (Leviticus 9:22-23)

We call this prayer in John 17 "the great high priestly
prayer" in part because we see all three of these priestly ob-
ligations revealed in Jesus' prayer here.

The Inward Emphasis of His Prayer

> Jesus looked up to heaven and said, "Father, the hour has come;
> glorify your Son so that the Son may glorify you, since you
> have given him authority over all people, to give eternal life
> to all whom you have given him. And this is eternal life, that
> they may know you, the only true God, and Jesus Christ whom
> you have sent. I glorified you on earth by finishing the work
> that you gave me to do. So now, Father, glorify me in your own
> presence with the glory that I had in your presence before the
> world existed."
> (vv. 1-5)

Just as the priest's prayer first makes confession so that
he might atone for his own sins, so our high priest, Jesus,
though he is without sin, begins his prayer by speaking of
his relationship with the Father. He is the mighty Christ but
he prays for assistance in this final prayer of his earthly ministry.

Previously we read, "They tried to arrest him, but no one
laid hands on him, because his hour had not yet come" (John
7:30). "He spoke these words while he was teaching in the
treasury of the temple, but no one arrested him, because his
hour had not yet come" (John 8:20). "His hour had not yet

come!" Those words are a signal to those around him that our Lord has come for an appointed moment on God's calendar and plan. As that moment arrives, he prays, "Father, the hour has come" (v. 1). Now that his time is here, Jesus seeks the Father's help that he might be faithful to the completion of his earthly ministry.

Why does Jesus pray like this? Because just up ahead looms the hardest part of his ministry on earth: His people will leave him, deny him, and some will run away from him. Pilate will treat him as a political pawn. His own people will call for the release of Barabbas, an incorrigible thief, over God's Son. On top of this, Gethsemane looms and the devil will be there to try to undo God's plan for the cross. He will plead in the Garden for another possibility. He knelt down, and prayed,

> "Father, if you are willing, remove this cup from me; yet, not my will but yours be done." Then an angel from heaven appeared to him and gave him strength. In his anguish he prayed more earnestly, and his sweat became like great drops of blood falling down on the ground.
> (Luke 22:41-44)

He prays for God the Father to make him sufficient for this hour that now has come.

Second, he prays to the Father about what he has achieved. "I glorified you on earth by finishing the work that you gave me to do" (v. 4). He has left his rightful place in heaven to set before the world an example of perfect living. He has not given in to Satan's temptations in the wilderness and he was tempted "in every respect... as we are, yet without sin" (Hebrews 4:15). He has healed the sick and raised the dead. But now death looms, not any ordinary death but the cruelest death that Rome's worst tyrants could imagine.

He has been clothed in human flesh for 33 years, and now he prays looking forward to his return to the glory that is his by right: "Father, glorify me in your own presence with the glory that I had in your presence before the world existed" (v. 5).

Our priest, Jesus, prays for himself, not because he is a sinner but because that is the method a priest follows when he enters the place of prayer.

The Upward Emphasis of His Prayer!

The upward focus of his prayer begins with a statement about the Father's glory. "He looked up to heaven and said, 'Father'... I glorified you on earth by finishing the work that you gave me to do" (vv. 1, 4). From Bethlehem to calvary, the Lord's ministry on earth has a singular emphasis. He reveals what God is like to people. Before Jesus, the best representation the people have is through the message of their religious leaders. It is harsh and judgmental and is essentially lacking in hope. Jesus brings a new vision of what God is like. John in the opening of his gospel says, "No one has ever seen God. It is God the only Son, who is close to the Father's heart, who has made him known" (John 1:18).

The upward focus of Jesus' prayer speaks next about the Father's genes. If you want to see God look at Jesus Christ. To Philip Jesus says: "Have I been with you all this time, Philip, and you still do not know me? Whoever has seen me has seen the Father. How can you say, 'Show us the Father' "? (John 14:9). Paul puts it this way: "He is the image of the invisible God, the firstborn of all creation" (Colossians 1:15). The Hebrew's writer uses these words, "He is the reflection of God's glory and the exact imprint of God's very being" (Hebrews 1:3). If you want to see God, look at Jesus. If you want to know what God thinks, get to know Jesus. In every way, he is God. How much like God the Father is Jesus? Consider this well-known statement: "God so loved the world that he gave his one and only Son" (John 3:16 NIV). Hidden in the middle of the Greek text is a powerful word *monogene*, a compound of the Greek words *mono*, meaning "the same," and *gene*, meaning "genetics." What Jesus is telling Nicodemus, and us, in this passage is that he and his Father share exactly the same genetic makeup. In other words, it would be impossible for Jesus to be any more like his Father than he is. No wonder then that Jesus says to Philip: "Whoever has seen me has seen the Father" (John 14:9).

Jesus next prays to his Father about his Father's gift: "I have made your name known to those whom you gave me from the world. They were yours, and you gave them to me" (v. 6). He is telling us that salvation is not received by human merit but that it is the act of the sovereign God who by grace saves us. Long before Jesus came to earth, David, under the Holy Spirit's influence, wrote: "The salvation of the righteous is from the Lord" (Psalm 37:39). Jesus has already said: "No one can come to me unless drawn by the Father who sent me; and I will raise that person up on the last day… For this reason I have told you that no one can come to me unless it is granted by the Father" (John 6:44, 65). Paul affirms this truth in his letter to the Ephesians: "By grace you have been saved through faith, and this is not your own doing; it is the gift of God" (Ephesians 2:8).

The final upward glance of the Lord's high priestly prayer calls for his Father's grace.

> I have made your name known to those whom you gave me from the world… the words that you gave to me I have given to them… Holy Father, protect them in your name that you have given me, so that they may be one, as we are one.
> (vv. 6, 8, 11)

Not only has God called them, and us, by his grace and for his glory, he also sustains us by his grace. We are what we are by God's grace. Paul knows this and writes,

By the grace of God I am what I am, and his grace toward me
has not been in vain. On the contrary, I worked harder than any
of them — though it was not I, but the grace of God that is with
me.
(1 Corinthians 15:10)

When we observe the lot of those less blessed than we are,
we often say, "There but for God's grace go I!" It is wonderfully true. Six centuries before Jesus was born Jeremiah
told us, "Because of the LORD's gracious love we are not
consumed, since his compassions never end" (Lamentations
3:22 ISV). So it is to be expected that Jesus, our great priest,
would ask the Father to continue his gracious protection and
direction toward us. Do you ever find yourself wondering
if God really does love you? Do you sometimes ask, "Do I
really matter to God?" Anytime you think like that in your
mind and heart, stop by again at calvary's cross. That cross
of Jesus is God's way of doing all he could do for us. Even
now he loves us and directs the circumstances of our lives
for our benefit. Paul writes: "We know that God causes all
things to work together for good to those who love God,
to those who are called according to *His* purpose" (Romans
8:28 NASB).

John Newton's great hymn "Amazing Grace" reminds us
each time we sing it:

...'Tis Grace that brought me safe thus far
And Grace will lead me home.

The Lord has promised good to me.
His word my hope secures.
He will my shield and portion be,
As long as life endures.

The upward impact of this marvelous prayer still takes
effect in the lives of God's own people. He is still protecting
us day-by-day.

The Outward Emphasis of His Prayer!

I have made your name known to those whom you gave me from the world. They were yours, and you gave them to me, and they have kept your word. Now they know that everything you have given me is from you; for the words that you gave to me I have given to them, and they have received them and know in truth that I came from you; and they have believed that you sent me. I am asking on their behalf; I am not asking on behalf of the world, but on behalf of those whom you gave me, because they are yours. All mine are yours, and yours are mine; and I have been glorified in them. And now I am no longer in the world, but they are in the world, and I am coming to you. Holy Father, protect them in your name that you have given me, so that they may be one, as we are one.
(vv. 6-11)

Having prayed with an inward emphasis and an upward emphasis, now Jesus prays with an outward emphasis.

He prays for the sustaining power of God on his people: "Holy Father, protect them in your name that you have given me, so that they may be one, as we are one" (v. 11). For 33 years, Jesus has lived a human life. He has experienced the meanness of this world. He knows its trials and struggles, having experienced them personally. He understands from of old the fall that Adam brought upon the human race. He knows that left to our own devices there are no downward limits to which we are incapable of falling. He is very much aware that none of us can maintain a wholesome relationship with God. That is why he prays for our protection and prays that the responsibility for our protection from ourselves and from the world in which we live be placed firmly with the Father. Peter considers this protection that is given to us and sings a doxology,

Blessed be the God and Father of our Lord Jesus Christ! By his great mercy he has given us a new birth into a living hope through the resurrection of Jesus Christ from the dead, and into

an inheritance that is imperishable, undefiled, and unfading, kept in heaven for you, who are being protected by the power of God through faith for a salvation ready to be revealed in the last time.
(1 Peter 1:3-5)

Because of this, we can live with the confidence that we are kept eternally secure in God's power.

I know that whatever God does endures forever; nothing can be added to it, nor anything taken from it; God has done this, so that all should stand in awe before him.
(Ecclesiastes 3:14)

Our Lord Jesus assures us,

My sheep hear my voice. I know them, and they follow me. I give them eternal life, and they will never perish. No one will snatch them out of my hand. What my Father has given me is greater than all else, and no one can snatch it out of the Father's hand. The Father and I are one.
(John 10:27-30)

Here is the glorious good news of the prayer that Jesus prays for us on this darkest of nights in his life. Our salvation is not dependent on our holding onto God, but on Christ Jesus our high priest securely holding onto us. "Consequently he is able for all time to save those who approach God through him, since he always lives to make intercession for them" (Hebrews 7:25).
To which we say, "Hallelujah! Amen!"

If You Like This Book...

Robert Leslie Holmes has also written the Pentecost-Second Third section titled "Bread and More! Forever! For Free!" for *Sermons on the Gospel Readings*, Series III, Cycle B (978-0-7880-2544-0) (printed book $37.95, e-book $29.95); and *Two Kings and Three Prophets for Less Than a Quarter*: First Lesson, Pentecost-Last Third, Cycle C (978-0-7880-1719-3) (printed book $12.95, e-book $9.95).

contact
CSS Publishing Company, Inc.
www.csspub.com
800-241-4056
orders@csspub.com

Prices are subject to change without notice.

CPSIA information can be obtained at www.ICGtesting.com
Printed in the USA
LVOW12s1622021113

359726LV00001B/4/P